ROLE PLAY

Personalities in Action

by

Julie Kembel

INC. TUCSON

Editor: Bonnie Marson
Cover design: David Fischer
Book design: Robert Kembel

ISBN 0-931836-52-2

Published by:

Northwest Learning Associates, Inc.
3061 N. Willow Creek Drive
Tucson, AZ 85712
520-881-0877, FAX: 520-881-0632

Printed in the United States of America

10 9 8 7 6 5 4 3 2

TABLE OF CONTENTS

All the world's a stage,
And all the men and women merely players;
They have their exits and their entrances,
And one man in his time plays many parts.

—William Shakespeare
As You Like It, Act II, Scene 7

Preface

This book is for all of you who have ever said: *If only I—you, he, she, we, they—were different, then everything would be perfect.* We are different, and that's the whole point. It's how we come together that makes, breaks, or troubles our significant relationships.

Diversity is all around us. It creates the technicolor in an otherwise black and white world. It brings variety and challenge, and gives us new dimensions. It excites us. While diversity may try our patience and undermine our security, it adds the spice to our lives.

Diversity is within us, too. It's what we depend on for the ability to shift gears with the needs of the moment, to respond appropriately to different people and situations. Diversity gives us our *persona*, the unique look and feel that separates us from others who have similar attitudes or behaviors. It also challenges our comfort with sameness and enables us to grow.

We rely on people's diversity to accomplish certain things, to add breadth and depth, to bring new ideas, methods, and skills. Magic happens when we blend our differences. I've certainly felt this magic in my reading and training in personality type, and in the creation of *ROLE Play*. So many people have contributed to this book. Most of them are unaware of it, but they're important nonetheless.

I am deeply indebted to people I have never met: Carl Jung (psychological theories), Katharine Briggs and Isabel Briggs Myers (MBTI personality type inventory), David Keirsey and Marilyn Bates (temperament theory), and the "edutainment" approach of Don Lowry (True Colors). Their contributions are legendary and they illuminate the path for all of us.

I am also indebted to people I have met. Some have been my teachers: Heather Alberts, Carol Ferlazzo, and Don Lawhead. Some have been my guides and co-developers: Kathryn Kellner, David Fischer, and Bonnie Marson. Some have given me a special vision: Nell Martin and Wayne

Nance. And one, my husband Bob, has been a mainstay of love and support in the long hours when fatigue or frustration overwhelmed me.

I have needed Kathryn's humor, knowledge, and guidance to help me write the narrative sections of this book. I've depended on Dave's insight and incredible talent to help me see more clearly and to bring the concepts to life in the character drawings. I've relied on Bonnie's wisdom and vision, and her own writing skills to make sure my words are clear, consistent, and correct. And Bob has used his own special "take" and talents to give this book its visual persona. Each person has contributed so much to me personally and professionally.

The foundation for this book comes from seven years of study and teaching experience with personality theory. Six exceptional people have been my teaching partners during this time: Nancy Arbas, Dan Baker, Chris Chapman, Suzanne Kaiser, Jodina Scazzola, and Catherine VanDeusen. Together we have brought the concepts and interplay of personality type to more than four thousand guests and employees of Canyon Ranch health and fitness resort in Tucson, Arizona. These participants have been a continual source of insight, knowledge, modeling, and advice. I have drawn upon their actions and reactions in writing this book. It's been great fun!

I am grateful to everyone who has touched me and my work in this field. Their individual personalities, perceptions, and suggestions appear everywhere in this book. Collectively these people represent the excitement and the magic of diversity!

Introduction

Quiet on the set! Lights ... Camera ... Action!

These words raise heart rates, focus attention, and propel all actors directly into role. Fantasy merges with reality as the performers infuse life into their characters with voice, gesture, facial expression, body motion, and costume. Actors use these tools to communicate a character's attitudes, values, and intentions which we then use to anticipate behavior.

Similarly, each of us has a distinct persona, or collection of predictable personality traits. These traits characterize us. We use specific language patterns and mannerisms, and have identifiable actions and reactions. We dress and move with a certain style. We convey our beliefs and values in typical ways that enable others to anticipate what we'll do and how we'll do it. People are most at ease when we do what's expected. When we behave strangely, they notice the difference and might say we're acting *out of character.*

We have all been taught to respond in certain ways. But, as with different actors who play the same part, we each bring a slightly different perspective to the same situation. When our perspectives are similar, conversation is comfortable and easy. When they are different, communication requires extra effort. As you learn more about character portrayal, you will:

- acquire useful insight about yourself and the people in your life

- learn how and why you relate to certain people as you do

- predict what people will do with greater accuracy

- understand what you can do to enhance the communication and connectedness in your relationships

Character and Personality

The concept of character as it is used in this booklet relates to well-defined personality types first described by Hippocrates in 400 B.C. Since then, many people have studied personality and written about its role in human behavior. Tools such as the Myers-Briggs Type Indicator help people assess personality by observing certain factors: interaction style; manner of obtaining and dealing with information; the basis for decisions; and approach to life. You may want to take this test for a deeper, more precise appraisal of your personality.

ROLE Play brings a dramatic flair to the topic of personality theory. Borrowing on the methods actors use to get into their roles, this book will help you recognize and relate to each personality type through the expression of a specific character. Each character has its own style and orientation. Pictures and descriptions will introduce you to each character's mind-set and behavior patterns. You will learn about the motivations and preferences which explain their attractions and aversions to certain people, tasks, conditions, and events. The intent of all of this is to help you:

- better understand yourself and others
- strengthen your compassion for people's differences
- increase your sensitivity and responsiveness to people's needs
- respect, appreciate, and use people's strengths and viewpoints
- communicate with others more effectively

The characters you will meet in this book embody the four main personality types and the roles they play in everyday life. They are symbolized by the words: **R**ational, **O**rganized, **L**oving, **E**nergized, and referred to by the letters: **R, O, L, E**. Look for these characters in yourself and the people around you. You'll see that *each of us is a blend of characters* with one or maybe two that stand out more strongly. You'll see how we use our characters to convey crucial information about ourselves, our needs and wants, our hopes and dreams, even our choices. You'll see how we use our knowledge of people's character preferences to predict their actions and reactions. As we learn to respond to the characters of the people we know, we gain comfort and confidence.

Getting into ROLE

Imagine you're going to audition for a part in a new play. What will you need to help you get into the role? Based on your learning style, you may rely more on facts, pictures, language, or feelings to obtain the necessary information and images. Then you can intellectualize, organize, relate, or create as needed to get into the character's mind, manner, and behavior.

The distinction here is that you already play a character—yourself. You have your own style, values, expectations, and behavior. And you live and work with other characters who have their own. How will you recognize and get along with everyone? How will you know how to assist, guide, influence, or oppose them? No matter how you learn best, there is something in *ROLE Play* to help you:

- **Character Cards** with engaging, insightful illustrations
- **Quizzes** for self-discovery
- **Character Studies** filled with interesting, useful information
- **Character Comparisons** for quick reference
- **Character Development** guidelines for personal growth
- **Reaching Out** techniques for better communication

Character Cards

These colorful character sketches paint clear pictures of people you meet every day. In our special deck of ROLE cards, you'll find detailed graphics that capture each character's style. The cards will give you quick visual clues to each character's preferences and values. You'll see how they like to appear, relate, work, and play. Which character fits you best?

Quiz Time

First Impression Quiz. You only get one chance at this quick-response word game! Peel away the adjectives that describe you to get a glimpse of your character. This quiz is on a separate page from the *ROLE Play* book

Second Look Quiz. First impressions are strong, but they don't tell the whole story. The Second Look Quiz gives a more rounded and detailed portrait of your character. You might be surprised by your own blend of character traits. You may notice your patterns are different at home than at work. If so, do the Character Quiz once in your business style, then do it again as your "at home" self.

Character Studies and Comparisons

The more you understand about a person, the better you can predict behavior and build rapport. Get to know each character's approach, attitudes, and aptitudes in the areas that matter most:

motivations and goals	communication
learning	dating, mating, and parenting
leadership and management	finances

Character Development

Actors change roles and so can you. At times you may want to give sincere expression to one of your less dominant characters. Learn how you can add breadth, depth, and flexibility to your strongest character by expanding the roles the other characters play. By using proven actor's techniques of concentration, visualization, and rehearsal, you can develop the less dominant characters in your profile and bring new options to your usual thinking and behavior.

Reaching Out

For empathy and insight, walk a mile in someone else's shoes. Try speaking with another character's language, using a different frame of reference. By understanding your own and other people's styles, you can find better ways to relate with and influence others.

Different Perspectives

Wouldn't it be dull if we were carbon copies of one another? Our similarities cause us to feel comfortable and secure; our differences fascinate and attract us, and challenge us to grow. The *ROLE Play* book and Character Cards have important information for you, no matter which character you play. Here's what the characters say:

R: *As the Rational character I'm interested in what you learn and its relevance in helping you achieve greater competence in your dealings with people. Here you will gain an appreciation for the big picture of human interaction. The background information is well-researched, accurate, and to the point. In a short time you will learn a great deal about human motivation and behavior.*

O: *As the Organized character I'm most interested in the practical details of what you learn and how you can apply it to your life. You will find this booklet to be well-organized with plenty of practical examples and clear, sensible suggestions. The information is easy to find and easy to use. Take advantage of the reference guides which give sound advice on techniques to help you improve your communication skills.*

L: *As the Loving character I am focused on the deeper meaning of this information. There is so much for you to learn! This book will help you gain new insight and deeper appreciation for yourself, to help you accept your uniqueness, and raise your self-esteem. It will help you take other people's actions less personally as you learn more about what inspires and rewards their behavior. I like the Character Studies and Backstage chapters best because I can hear each character's words and feel as though I'm getting to know them more intimately.*

E: *As the Energized character I like information to be fun, action-oriented, and immediately practical. There's lots of fun stuff here! Have a character party and give the cards and quiz to everyone. They'll love it. The Character Comparisons chapter is cool. I use it to check out my perceptions of my friends. The book is full of great ideas to help you be more flexible, think better on your feet, and add impact to what you say and do.*

Character Cards

The Character Cards provide a quick visual perspective of each personality type in four dimensions. Notice the cards are printed on both sides. Use the drawings to familiarize yourself with each of the characters: **R**ational, **O**rganized, **L**oving, **E**nergized. The cards capture the image and spirit of the characters. They show the visual look and feel of each character, and how each of them likes to appear, relate, work, and play.

Sorting the Cards

1. Choose two categories to work with first. Lay the Character Cards out in front of you, placing all cards in each category in a horizontal row. **Place all Work cards in one horizontal row, for example, and all Play cards in a second row. This lets you see the big picture of each character's orientation within a single category and, at the same time, begin to identify yourself.**

2. Now arrange the cards in the order of their relevance to you.
   a) **Within each row place the card that most strongly identifies you on the left.**
   b) **From the remaining three cards place the one in each row that most strongly describes you to the right of the first card.**
   c) **Continue until all cards have been arranged. You will have two horizontal rows arranged by categories; and four vertical columns arranged by preference, column 1 on the left with the cards that most strongly describe you and column 4 on the right with the cards that most weakly describe you.**

3. Using either the letters or colors as your guide, notice which characters show up most often in columns 1 and 2. **Record the total number of cards for each character in these two columns.**

4. Now turn all the cards over and repeat steps 1 through 3.

Interpreting the Results

The sorting and counting will give you the first and most general orientation to your preferred style. You probably had a blend of characters in the first two columns. This is typical, because we are truly a combination of personalities.

Look at the number totals for each of the characters. The character with the highest total represents your strongest preference; the one with the lowest total represents your weakest.

You may find that you have a numerical tie between two characters. Or one character is only one or two points lower than another. Maybe you didn't put one or two of the characters in the first two columns at all and therefore you didn't record any numbers for them. Don't worry about all of this right now. You'll be able to assess yourself more deeply and accurately later on.

The purpose of this first visual orientation is to help you familiarize yourself with the different characters and to begin to identify your own style within the categories. Use these cards and the sorting process with friends, family members, and colleagues. It will help all of you recognize some of the commonalities and differences among you and lead you into discussions about your respective thoughts and feelings. This, in turn, will open the door to greater understanding, appreciation, and acceptance of one another.

Second Look Quiz

Up to this point you have been gathering general impressions about yourself. Now it's time for a second look to see whether your first impressions are accurate. Take a few moments right now to think more deeply about yourself—as you see yourself *most of the time.* Then read the directions and do the quiz on the back of this page.

Are you very different at work than you are at home? If so, choose one setting at a time when you do this quiz. In other words, do the quiz once and focus on yourself in your work mode; then do the quiz in your at-home mode. There are no right or wrong choices in this quiz, only preferences for how you like to function best.

Begin with the left-hand column. Read the opening phrase. Select the word in the same row that fits you most accurately and write a 4 next to it. In that same row, choose the word that fits you next best; write a 3 alongside it. Then designate 2 and 1.

Give every word in each row a number and use each number only once within a row. You will have to make choices, some of which may be difficult. Go with your gut feeling about what reflects you *as you are* rather than how you wish you could be.

Stop reading now and do the quiz. Then return to this page and read on. When ready, enter your character profile below:

_____ _____ _____ _____

Add the numbers in each column and write the totals on the bottom row. The column with the highest number indicates your strongest preference; the one with the lowest indicates your weakest. Which character belongs to each column? Beginning with the left column and moving to the right, they are ROLE. Put this information on the character profile above, writing the letter of the strongest character on the left and the weakest on the right. Does this fit your initial impressions? Or the Character Cards? Your choices may not fit exactly and that's OK. You're learning more with each exercise.

I am	logical	practical	idealistic	creative
I focus on	facts	tasks	people	action
I need	objectivity	order	harmony	challenge
I am often	quiet	busy	passionate	enthusiastic
People say I am	smart	dedicated	inspiring	free-spirited
I search for	competence	security	significance	excitement
I tend to be	reserved	efficient	caring	charming
I respect	accuracy	authority	feelings	freedom
I dislike	repetition	waiting	selfishness	pressure
At home I am	problem-solver	rule-maker	listener	playmate
At work I am best at	seeing the big picture	getting things done	motivating people	generating new ideas
When dealing with problems I usually	seek more information	focus on the details	offer emotional support	take immediate action
I have a lot of	natural wit	common sense	love	energy
I value	fairness	tradition	personal growth	pleasure
I can be	skeptical	intense	too sensitive	restless
I am seen as being	thorough	predictable	gentle	the life of the party
I am a	thinker	planner	dreamer	doer
I need to have	standards	procedures	affirmation	options
I am annoyed by	illogical people	messy people	rude people	negative people
When making decisions I	weigh the pros and cons	think of what must be done	talk with others	come up with quick answers
I am irritated by	irrelevant conversation	failure to follow rules	impersonal treatment	rules and regulations
I dislike	rapid change	wasting time	conflict	deadlines
I am sometimes	sarcastic	bossy	emotional	flighty
TOTAL POINTS				

Character Studies

In the world of stage and screen, Character Studies provide the essential information actors need to learn about the background, traits, and motivations of their characters. Two actors who audition for the same part receive the same written information which gives the character consistency. But what distinguishes one portrayal from another is the unique twist each actor brings to the character.

Each day you encounter different characters as they are played by the people around you. While everyone portrays their dominant character a bit differently, they still follow a definable pattern. In other words, each character has its own template that enables you to distinguish it no matter who plays it. Since all characters have a role in your life, the more you know about their needs, motivations, actions, and idiosyncrasies, the easier it will be to relate to them.

The Character Studies in this chapter are written in the characters' own voices, using words and language patterns that are indicative of each one's overall style. Don't assume that all people of a single character speak identically. The characterizations simply offer a way for you to become acquainted with each of them more personally. And the content will give you a broader, deeper picture of each character's intentions and behavior.

What will you learn? You'll learn about each character's:

- motivations and goals
- learning and communication patterns
- dating, mating, and parenting behavior
- leadership and management styles
- financial preferences

Use the Character Studies to gain deeper insight about what drives and rewards each of them, and to learn how to respond to them in ways that capture their attention and earn their respect. In time you'll become comfortable with the characters and increasingly able to be more "in sync" with each one's language, thoughts, and typical responses. Then you can build a common ground for communication and establish rapport more quickly.

The best way to approach these Character Studies is to concentrate on one at a time, beginning with your own dominant character.

- Read the information once to gain the overall nature of the personality. Allow yourself to form general impressions.
- Read the Character Study again, this time looking for significant details.
- Underline key words and phrases or make notes to yourself in the margins for quick recall or review.

Depending on your own learning style, you may prefer to browse through all of the Character Studies at once and return to them later, when you're ready for more specific information. Do whatever suits you best.

The R Character

I am Rational. I think the name explains all you need to know to get the essence of who I am—the rest can be extrapolated from the meaning of the word, rational. But I will elaborate in order to make certain concepts clearer. I am logical, conceptual, objective, and dispassionate. I appreciate a good mental challenge, and find it quite easily on my own. I read and study. I look up information. I think about what I've read and examine the interrelationships among different facts and concepts. I remember everything. So don't imagine that I forget the things you tell me, though I may choose not to comment on them.

I'm self-sufficient. That is, I take care of my own needs, solve my own problems, and provide entertainment and companionship for myself. I like this aspect of my character. I'm also independent in terms of my thoughts and actions. I rarely seek other people's opinions or advice unless there is good reason for me to do so. It's not that I feel superior to other people or I'm uninterested in what they think; it is more that I prefer to do my own thinking and form my own opinions first. I am meticulous about gathering reliable information and exceedingly careful about thinking things through before making decisions. All of this takes time which frustrates other people and causes them to think I am procrastinating but I assure you, this impression is inaccurate.

I'm a person who likes to be in control at all times. I like order and quiet. Therefore, I avoid situations that call for spontaneity or emotional reactivity. When I'm confronted with circumstances of this nature, I withdraw and become physically and emotionally detached. I conceal my emotions with impersonal, objective thoughts and, in this way, I'm able to retain my composure.

I'm rarely at a loss for interesting things to do. I enjoy tinkering with my computer, browsing the network data banks for information, discovering new applications, and entertaining myself with interesting programs and intellectually challenging games. Yes, I'm a computer nerd, which scores many points with the computer-illiterate people who rely on my help. I also tinker with electronic gadgets, and even invent a few of my own!

Motivations and Goals

I challenge myself to be competent in all things. I like to win. Winning not only means I have excelled—which is important to me—it also means I've figured out how to do it which means I can win again. You see, I focus on process as well as facts.

I am perpetually curious and have a phenomenal memory, two factors which give me a decided advantage over other characters. I'm not easily distracted either, so I can stay focused on what I'm doing no matter what's going on around me. Others tell me that I ignore them but the truth is, I don't really notice them. I don't allow myself to become scattered.

There is more to me than winning, learning, and remembering. I strive to be fair and just. I'm painstakingly thorough. I take as much time as I need to carefully examine all pertinent facts and weigh the impact of all decisions before taking action. Once made, my decisions are firm.

My goals are objective and precise. I am most interested in what will be achieved and how it will affect my life overall. I've been told that I am too future-focused and global in scope, that I ignore practical details. Personally, I think too many people miss the forest for the trees.

Learning

Knowledge is very important to me. I have infinite patience for studying the why and how of things. I learn by reading, analyzing, synthesizing, and applying. I challenge everyone and everything. I learn best this way, so please realize that when I take exception to something you said, it's not a personal attack. I love a great debate!

I admit, I'm a skeptic. I don't accept things on face value. I'd rather research and analyze the facts and background information for myself. I detest being spoonfed! I respect instructors who present their information logically and concisely, and who show me how the study assignments fit into the overall plan. Without this, I'm resistant. I like to work with charts and graphs because they allow me to grasp, compute, and compare information quickly. I am usually quiet in a group setting.

Communication   R

I am the most focused communicator of all the characters. I rarely engage in idle chatter. I get to the point quickly and avoid repetition. In groups I'm usually more content to listen than participate but when a response is called for, I can be clever and entertaining.

Like other Rs, I need to see the big picture before I can focus on the details. This is true in conversations, too. I want you to give me the overview first, then present the details objectively and clearly. I have no patience for hearsay or emotional rhetoric. I like to remain calm and intellectually unbiased until I have heard and processed all relevant information. To be most fair to you, I want to grasp the projected impact of your issues as well as the implications for action.

I tend to speak in theoretical and complex terms. I don't try to be pedantic, it's just my way. I'm so attuned to verbal precision that I don't often notice whether the listener grasped my words or concepts. I expect people to speak up when they need clarification.

Like other Rs, I'm a natural linguist. I continually explore the nuances of language and enjoy baiting others with obscure words. Apparently this annoys certain people who find it necessary to complain that I am condescending. Rubbish! I simply like to play word games.

In terms of my communication style, I am more verbally than physically expressive. I use fewer facial expressions and physical gestures than other characters. People who rely on visual clues for measuring my reactions tell me I am inscrutable. I am usually unaware of my physical self which, I'm sure, makes me appear to be detached—aloof, according to my mother.

I meet new ideas with skepticism which unfortunately arouses people's insecurities to the degree that some of them refuse to discuss new concepts or untested theories with me. This disappoints me, because I learn by challenging everything which includes ideas, facts, and feelings. There is nothing personal in this. As long as people remain calm and present their views logically, I hear them even when the information is personal rather than factual. I will entertain any idea or discussion topic that is thought out well and presented objectively.

People tell me they have more trouble building personal relationships with Rs than with other characters. As I think about it, I realize I have few close friends. This doesn't bother me because I'm quite content with my own company. But it does seem to worry other people—especially the socially conscious types who insist the problem resides in my overly complex nature which makes me too incomprehensible for others to understand or relate to. Maybe so. I'll have to think about that.

Life with me is calm, predictable, and stable. I like routine. I prefer to eat in the same restaurants, for example. I like to follow the same route to and from work and watch the same things on television. To others this may be boring but I have little need for external variety or excitement.

I detest arguments and emotional outbursts. I think they're more hurtful than helpful. I believe in fairness and personal restraint, so I support brief discussions that focus on facts. But sometimes conflicts are unavoidable. I hold myself more strongly accountable for all arguments that involve me, and therefore assume most of the responsibility for resolving the problems.

I don't share my feelings easily or often. I'm an intensely private person. I will not discuss personal problems with others nor divulge confidential information about the people in my life. I keep silent about business relationships, too. This irritates the inquisitive types who always want to know intimate details, but gossip is offensive to me. People who know me well accept my ethical standards and respect me for being circumspect.

I don't chatter. I don't say "I love you" often enough. Like most Rs, I dislike repeating myself or stating what seems perfectly obvious to me. I rarely send flowers. Additionally, I may forget to give cards or gifts on special occasions. I don't mean to be rude or neglectful. I don't need these things myself and am amazed by the importance people give to such tokens.

I have deep attachments to only a few people and I take these commitments seriously. I provide for my parents, my present (and previous) mate, and my children. I am a concerned, involved parent. I like to share my interests and hobbies and engage my children in mentally stimulating activities. I am reliable, helpful, patient, objective, and fair.

Leadership and Management   R

In business, competence says more to me than authority, credentials, or popularity. I'm a strong individualist and neither want nor need other people's opinions. I'd rather analyze situations myself than rely on advice or precedent. I trust my ability to think strategically and systemically.

I have a reliable talent for seeing details at the big picture level so I am invaluable in creating an organization's mission statement and conceptual plans. As for the practical details of carrying out these plans, I prefer to delegate them to other characters who are better suited to such tasks.

I hear that I make things more complicated than necessary. This may be true. I'm a stickler for competent performance. I expect a great deal from myself and others, and am irritated by incomplete, inaccurate, or careless workmanship. I am not an ogre, though. I don't dispense praise casually but I do let people know when they've performed exceptionally well.

My formal, exacting manner can put people off, though I don't intend to make others uncomfortable. My caustic wit can be hard on gentler people who may feel I'm picking on them. This is unfortunate. I think people need to develop a stronger ego and not take everything I say so personally.

Employees find me to be impartial and fair, and steady in direction and mood. While I'm more focused on issues than feelings, I do offer a listening ear when someone needs an objective sounding board. When talking to me, just get to the point quickly. You'll lose me with rambling conversations.

I encourage employees to think and solve problems themselves. I like to see people become more independent, able to reason and use their intellect, and make decisions logically. I respect employees' efforts to learn and become more professionally competent. I also respect employees' efforts to bring new ideas and methods to my attention.

In meetings, I'm usually quiet. I listen, watch, and think. I like meetings that follow agendas because it minimizes disruptions, digressions, and irrelevant chatter. I speak only when I have something valuable to add, though I do contribute quips and somewhat caustic repartee. So you see, I do have a playful side!

Finances   R

Like most Rs, I'm inspired more by the challenge of making money than the security of having it or the pleasure of showing it off. Wealth attests to my competence at winning the money game. I prefer to manage most of my investments myself and continually look for new ways to "beat the system." I read the financial pages daily and monitor performance with computer-generated reports. I often use computer networks to identify, track, and trade the products in my portfolio.

I am content to live modestly. I have few material wants except for my books, technological tools, and favorite electronic gadgets. Since I plan to work rather than retire in the customary sense, I worry less than other people about stockpiling large sums of money for the future.

I'm a tough customer for investment counselors. I read. I investigate. I am attuned to large-scale patterns so I'm able to anticipate the direction companies, governments, and financial institutions will take. I frequently know more than the experts who contact me. I have no patience for sales pitches, incomplete or inaccurate information, or bluffing. I do respect people who have done their homework and who get back to me with needed information. I will listen to brief, well-organized presentations, and do appreciate a "heads up" from someone I respect about a worthwhile tip or an impending change.

I am meticulous about updating my financial records and budget. I keep all of this information in my computer and make backup copies regularly in case of system malfunction. I'm prudent. I recognize the value of estate planning and do have the necessary documents completed and filed as appropriate. I also maintain an inventory of household items for insurance purposes.

I tend to underinsure my life and possessions. I'm skeptical of the value of many kinds of insurance and tend to reject policies with large dollar values. I'd rather invest my money in funds with some liquidity that can be tapped to meet emergency needs. I'm conservative in most things. I need time to study my options and resent being pressured to make hasty decisions. In summary, I am astute, self-reliant, and deliberate.

The O Character

I am an O which stands for orderly, obedient, obliging, and organized. I like to be of service to others and to the organizations I am connected with. I'm very organized and, from an operations perspective, I get things done. I'm also opinionated—too much so for some people's comfort. But then, everyone knows exactly where I stand on most things. This avoids confusion and the need to second-guess which really wastes a lot of time and energy. If we all could be more direct and keep each other informed, the world would be a better run, happier place to live. Don't you agree?

As I see it, life is serious business and I feel responsible for making sure everything runs smoothly. In fact, I focus so much on getting things done that I often appear to be uptight which, I think, is overstated. I'm simply focused and not easily distracted. I take enormous pride in a job well done.

I honor and uphold the good, old-fashioned values of thrift, hard work, honesty, and community service. I'm a worker bee, which more critical people might reframe as a workaholic. The truth is, to me work is play and play is work. I find satisfaction in my work and have few reservations about donating my private time to finish an important project. I like to have meaningful things to do so even my hobbies have a useful aspect. I knit, sew, garden, play with my children, and do my physical exercise according to schedule. I won't just sit around with nothing to do.

I'm a practical person, sensible and down-to-earth. I rarely take risks with anything. I like routine. I especially enjoy holiday and family celebrations that have a proscribed ritual to them—certain foods, decorations, activities, and expectations. I'm not terribly adventurous and the sameness of these events gives me a great feeling of security.

Like other Os, I'm efficient and punctual. I use lists, plans, calendars, and time lines to help me manage my home and my work. And when I plan my vacation, I have all reservations made and often paid for in advance so there are no last-minute surprises. When the agenda calls for play, I play with the same focus and dedication I use at work. I can be spontaneous within a set structure which means I work well with defined options.

Motivations and Goals   O

As an O, my strongest motivator is security so punctuality, predictability, and structure are necessary to me. I'm cautious and conservative because this feels safe. I'm uneasy with change because it feels unknown, unclear, uncontrolled—all conditions that arouse my insecurity.

I like to plan ahead so I can be properly prepared. Unanticipated problems unnerve me so I usually have contingency plans in place. All of this worry makes other people think I'm stressed-out and pessimistic but to me, being prepared is half the battle.

My goals are direct, well-defined, and measurable. I set them quickly so I can get started on implementing them. I dislike revising goals when it means re-doing work I've already done. I hate to waste time! My idea of a good day is finishing everything on my list and being ahead of schedule.

Learning   O

Like other Os, I enjoy learning, especially when the subject has a practical aspect. I want to do something concrete with what I learn. I especially like self-study projects that allow me to gather facts and organize information.

I'm a self-starter and a task-completer. I work very hard. I listen well and take good notes during lectures. I like visual aids that make the concepts clearer. I grasp information best when it is presented visually as well as verbally. I do well with charts, graphs, diagrams, and illustrations.

I strive to do things correctly, motivated as I am by the acceptance and approval I need to feel secure. For this reason I like to have clearly defined goals and performance expectations, as well as schedules, assignments, and due dates. This allows me to plan ahead.

Unlike many people, I become anxious when I don't understand something right away. When this happens, I can't relax or focus on anything else until someone explains it to me or I can work it through for myself.

I need to feel successful. I respond well to rewards and recognition for my efforts. I appreciate helpful suggestions and supportive feedback.

Communication   O

I strive to be correct in what I say and how I say it, and try very hard to be appropriate at all times. Etiquette and courtesy are important attributes that I respect in others and demand in myself. Whether I'm tipping a cab driver, holding an infant, or speaking to people in their native language, I want to do it properly.

I'm a direct, matter-of-fact communicator. I like to get to the point quickly to conserve time. Like other Os, I process information and make decisions promptly. I become impatient, then angry when people procrastinate, especially in decision-making. I may seem to be harsh and overly critical at such times, but this stems from my urgency to bring things to closure. Once I understand that certain people require more processing time, I'll make the necessary allowances so everyone can feel comfortable.

People tell me I'm too serious. I don't chatter or make jokes, that's true. I talk about situations and things. I have an earnest style that feels formal and may come across as stuffy. This frustrates me because I admire other people's spontaneity. I wish I could be more easygoing. When people talk with me on a feeling level, I respond with genuine warmth and concern. I strive to be helpful. I give advice. Sometimes my take-charge approach conveys an attitude of control or intensity that makes people feel uneasy. This is simply a consequence of my desire to expedite things and not a wish to assume ownership.

In my business mode, I'm conscientious, clear, and well-organized. I furnish careful, point-by-point explanations. I sometimes hear that I give people more information than they need, but I believe in being thorough. I like to operate meetings from a written agenda, which I send to people in advance so they can be ready to address and resolve all of the items. I try to involve everyone in the discussions. I am a skillful meeting facilitator.

My typical communication style is purposeful. I watch and listen intently which makes me seem intense. While my manner is more businesslike, when the agenda calls for humor and play, I respond with the same focus and dedication I apply to my work. Beneath my somewhat severe exterior, I am a warm, genuine person who wants to be liked and accepted.

Dating, Mating, and Parenting   O

Socially, I'm rather conservative. I follow precedent. I embrace traditions and ceremonies because they give me a feeling of continuity. I like social gatherings. I enjoy planning and preparing. I don't even mind cleaning up. I assume responsibility for making sure everything runs well and that everyone in the group has met one another. I think I'm a friendly, considerate person.

Like many Os, I have lifelong friends with whom I keep in touch regularly. I'm very loyal and stand by my friends and family even when others disapprove. Sometimes my loyalty causes problems, because I can be unreasonably jealous when people who are close to me show more attention to others than to me. This is a security issue. I have a strong need to belong and feel accepted, so I'm more easily hurt when I think I've been excluded.

I honor commitments. I follow rules. I strive to be faithful to my marriage vows. Once married, I put fantasy and romance aside and get down to the practicality of work, home, family, and friends. I am rarely bored in my relationships. I'm content with regularity and prefer emotional stability to the uncertainty of greater excitement.

Arguments upset me. No matter who the person is, I want to resolve the issues quickly. I'm willing to listen to feelings, but I need to have closure on the important issues and a concrete plan for achieving resolution. I can be quite a nag about this because I don't like to leave things up in the air, especially when it affects my relationships with the people I care about.

I am very involved in family activities. I invest plenty of time and effort in talking with, teaching, helping, and supporting my children. I monitor what my young children watch on TV because I want them to form proper values. I organize family outings, arrange for lessons, plan family celebrations, and manage the routine details of family life.

I actively support the activities and organizations my children are involved in. I volunteer to help at school functions and sports events. I want my children to feel loved and secure, and to know by my actions that they are important to me. I also make certain that family rules and curfews are adhered to. I raise my children to be obedient, polite, and self-sufficient.

What would the working environment be like without people like me? Who would make sure everything gets done? Who would attend to the policies and procedures? Who would have the patience to deal with the details of organizational design and day-to-day operations?

Like other Os, I'm a prolific designer of organizational structures—the charts, graphs, assignments, schedules, budgets, rules, and regulations needed to run businesses and deliver products. I plan and manage projects extremely well. I'm keenly aware of what's going on, what needs to be done, and who to contact for information or assistance.

People tell me I'm a workaholic. I don't understand that. I admit I am unable to ignore unfinished tasks, even when I already have a full plate. It's not that I want to be a martyr, or that I'm unwilling to delegate work to others. I simply believe in doing a good job and fulfilling my obligations. I'm very responsible and just can't leave things hanging. Besides, it feels good to be needed; it helps me feel more secure. So much of who I am is tied up in my work.

I'm a take-charge person. I dislike indecision and dawdling. I'd rather do things myself. I'm focused, efficient; accurate, thorough, and productive. I'm conscious of other people's opinions and strive to run a tight ship at all times. I have a commonsense approach to everything I do. I am cautious, so I rarely take risks. I review precedent and weigh the probable consequences prior to making decisions.

I like to work with people, especially in the areas of staff training and development. Employees see that I'm interested in their ideas and attentive to their needs and achievements. I expect and reward hard work. I do performance evaluations on schedule, and allot extra time to develop, discuss, and agree on performance objectives for the subsequent appraisal period. I help my employees build strong, effective teams.

Employees always know where they stand with me for I give ready praise or discipline as needed. I expect my staff to be punctual, loyal, obedient, dedicated, and appropriate in manner and attire. I initiate and perpetuate traditions so we all have a feeling of belonging and continuity.

I am cautious in most things and prudent in my spending habits. I buy things on sale whenever possible and pay for things as I go along. I take pride in maintaining a positive credit rating and avoiding unnecessary debt. I use a budget to track expenses. I always add extra money to my mortgage payment to reduce the principal. I intend to have my house paid for well ahead of schedule.

Do you remember a savings bank commercial whose slogan was, "Pay yourself first?" I thought that was, and still is, a very important message. I don't understand why our government penalizes people for saving money and rewards them for debt. That's backward to me. I never charge more than I can pay for in 30 days. I've never had a finance charge for anything except my car and the mortgage on my home—and I'm proud of it.

Overall, I am a practical person. I buy serviceable items from stores with good repair and returns policies. I read consumer reviews before making large purchases. I'm not extravagant and readily cut corners to save money, but I strive to buy quality items of lasting value.

As I've said earlier, I have strong security needs. I worry continually about my financial future. I set money aside for education, vacations, and emergencies. I rarely take risks. I'm interested in wills, trusts, retirement plans, and all types of insurance. I like predictable investments even though they may be less profitable. I get very upset when my investments lose money. I feel most comfortable with bank accounts, mutual funds, bonds, and CDs.

Unlike Rs, I don't need to see the big picture, just the specifics of what must be done next. I'm a concrete, business-like person. I need to know exactly what is required of me. I like to have written goals, detailed instructions, and plans, products, and reports that allow me to measure my progress. I am easily over-whelmed when I'm given too many options to consider at one time. I do best with a few well-chosen products to review.

I resent sales agents who sell me a product and never contact me again. I want regular follow-up. I respond best to guidance from someone whose reputation, credentials, and behavior earn my respect.

The L Character

We are the caring, relational optimists who firmly believe in the intrinsic worth of every living being. We love people and value our relationships with them. We want people to feel comfortable around us. We want them to know we all have wonderful qualities and potential. People say they feel affirmed and appreciated when they're with us. This makes us feel good.

Every day we see people in need. We all do. Ls can't ignore them. We feel that our most important gifts as human beings are compassion and sensitivity without judgment. We don't understand why others don't live this way. How devastating for people to be left alone in a time of need! We can't do that. Friends say we hover over them too much and should focus more on ourselves. Maybe so. We do put people's needs ahead of our own which sometimes leaves us feeling emotionally exhausted.

Conflict upsets us. Hurtful arguments don't help anyone and they don't solve problems. We seek harmony. We'll comply with others' wishes if it makes them feel better. We champion the underdog. People tell us we're naive but we firmly believe everyone has potential and deserves a chance to make a difference in the world. We're not weak, and we're not pushovers. We simply want everyone to be happy.

Ls believe good will is more important than winning a battle or scoring a point. We don't have a "dog eat dog" attitude and, frankly, we're outraged at those who do. We all need each other. Everyone contributes something valuable to the human experience. Perhaps we're idealistic. But we like our idealism—and our spirituality, too. We believe we can have a society of happy, loving people who play and work together in harmony, regardless of their differences. What's the true meaning of life if it isn't getting along and sharing our truths without conflict.

People say we shouldn't approach everything from a personal value system and should use our intellect to solve problems. Without values how can we impact the people who exploit others or destroy our natural resources to gratify their own wants? We need values and mutual respect to change the condition of our world and support the welfare of all who live here.

Motivations and Goals   L

Are you getting the idea that we Ls are motivated by relationships and global responsibility? You're right. And we're motivated by self-discovery, too. We seek to know who we are and to understand our roles in life. We are characteristically interactional and learn about ourselves through our connections with the universe, nature, and other people. We want the best, and the most, for everyone. We believe in people's intrinsic worth and the sanctity of life. We strive to be in harmony with ourselves and others.

We are idealistic goal-setters. We are more global than detailed in scope. You will hear our goals expressed more creatively than practically, in language that tends to be more abstract and difficult to measure. We strive for consensus when preparing group-oriented goals, and we choose more feeling words than other characters typically use.

We are humanists. We think about the impact that meeting our goals will have on other people. No matter how global our goals, we can be focused in our efforts. You will find many of us in your own communities working in the nitty-gritty of everyday life, supporting the causes that improve the quality of life for everyone.

Learning   L

We value the personal aspect of learning. We're creative and imaginative. Look on our bookshelves and you'll find volumes on self-help, inspiration, and metaphysical teachings. We want to know how things relate to us. More than that, we want to know how we can use our knowledge to help others. We like sharing what we've learned. Discussion is the most stimulating and important part of learning as far as we are concerned.

In school, our teachers typically think we ask too many personal questions about other students' experiences and ideas. We probably do. We like the cooperative exchange of ideas because it fosters human potential. We thrive in situations where people share their different perspectives. We have been called interpersonal learners. We like that! We love to harvest the ideas that others have grown and blend them all into a recipe for living.

Communication   L

People readily come to us just to talk. They are drawn to our warmth and openness, and to our affirming style. We genuinely like people and draw energy from being with them. Isolation doesn't suit us.

Ls have a natural flair for language and we delight in using prose, poetry, music, and metaphor to convey personal meaning. But our best asset is our listening skills. We are sensitive to spoken and unspoken feelings. We're artful in sorting out other people's perspectives and helping them resolve their issues. We honor and respect truthfulness, even when someone else's truth is different from our own. We appreciate sincerity.

We like to add a personal touch to all of our communication. We love to give special gifts and handwritten notes. We tell people how much we appreciate them and the things they've done. We cherish kindness and caring. We believe in letting people know they are valued.

When we have to communicate formally, we like to begin with a conceptual perspective. We feel that insight and creativity are stifled when people start off with too many details. In negotiations, we try to highlight the points of agreement early and resist the pressure to reach closure too quickly. We believe it's better for everyone when there's time to process things and consider the potential impact of the various options.

Ls are often asked to mediate in conflict situations. We have the traits that make us skilled communicators. We like to to "go with the flow." This kind of flexibility lets us hear and respond to people without the encumbrance of our own agenda. This works well in situations where we want to make the best use of the information that emerges from everyone's interaction.

The symbolic word for our style of communication is bonding. We try to establish rapport. We like people to smile, be calm, and look at us directly. When people look away, get upset, or close up their bodies with folded arms, we feel rejected. Then our feelings get stirred up and we lose focus. We feel most supported when people are genuine, honest, and affirming—and especially when they're willing to hear and respond to our concerns. It is hard for us to ask for what we want so we need others to reach out to us.

Ls are true romantics. We seek pure love. We want complete understanding, total commitment, and unconditional acceptance. We know this sounds too good to be true, but why not seek the best? When we are in love, we express ourselves emotionally, physically, and spiritually. To live or die for love is a sentiment we relate to. Don't misunderstand, we're not totally out of touch with reality. But we are idealists. We give our all to our relationships.

People say we shouldn't go overboard in our zeal to experience total, loving fulfillment. When we do, we lose sleep, reason, and perspective. We become overly sensitive to people's reactions, and begin to imagine we're disliked or rejected. We feel deeply so we hurt deeply, too. We need genuine support and caring from others to regain our perspective and composure.

We believe in the inherent goodness of people, which allows us to have extraordinary patience. We tolerate actions and situations that turn others off. Of all the characters, we Ls are most likely to linger in unrewarding relationships because we trust things will get better. We do have limits, though, and we'll end a relationship that's become too painful. Some of us move from person to person, searching for someone who will go the distance and not fade in commitment or focus over time. It's so frustrating to give so much and be left with so little!

The fallout of our idealism is that we take things too personally. We cling to others. Some of us brood, some cry, and some become emotional victims. We want forgiveness and love. We need attention and approval from our family and friends. In time, we regain self-esteem and emotional resilience.

As parents, we appreciate our children. We give them affection, support, and affirmation. We teach them about acceptance and forgiveness. We encourage them to be sensitive and develop their potential. Our children are at the center of our lives. We love to listen to their stories and share their experiences. We often set aside our needs or defer our personal growth to be available for them. Many of us become enmeshed in our children's lives and suffer when they leave home or no longer need our help. We must be encouraged to pursue our own interests.

Leadership and Management

We love to work with people and are often given leadership responsibilities. People tell us we have charisma. We are attuned to our employee's needs and deeply committed to their welfare. It seems to us that we're often the only ones who have a handle on the emotional climate at work. We feel that happy employees are central to business success, so we give them time, attention, and support. We're staunch advocates of personal and professional growth, and encourage everyone to develop their potential. We've been told we have the perfect outlook for teaching, counseling, and human resources. We agree. We Ls thrive in careers that draw on our extraordinary gifts for communication and collaboration.

We expect cooperation from our employees and fellow managers. We strive to instill harmony in the work environment. We want people to be respectful of one another's feelings and needs. We want them to be honest, even when we might not like what they'll say. People need to express their views without fear of retribution. We're attentive and available to those we supervise, and we're receptive to hearing about personal as well as work-related issues. After all, we deal with the whole person. But we've been criticized for allowing employees to become dependent. We think it's difficult to maintain appropriate boundaries with everyone.

Most Ls love meetings. It's a time for sharing feelings and ideas. We like to facilitate group discussion and help everyone arrive at consensus. This requires time, though, and patience. We want to listen to everyone's views before making decisions that affect people's lives or the company's well-being. So we take time and make decisions slowly, a trait that annoys and frustrates other people. We do feel badly about that but it's how we operate.

We are focused more on people and process than deadlines and details so we have to be reminded to do our paperwork. Most of us start our day with intent to do desk projects but we're continually interrupted by people who need our time and attention. So, another day passes and the paper piles up. We can't throw anything away, either so our desks are covered with things to read and do. We give so much to our jobs that we're often overstretched and overtired. Burnout is a familiar word to us. We know we should review our priorities and set limits for ourselves. It's just hard to say "no."

Finances   L

Money doesn't mean much to us. Oh, we like to have money, but we generally give it away. Actually, we look at money as an investment in humankind. Most Ls like to use their financial resources to help people, to improve their quality of life, provide financial security, or support a mission that touches the heart. What's money for if not to help others?

We Ls aren't sophisticated money managers. We stash bills and coins in odd places, and in envelopes designated for special purposes—"nest eggs" as people call them. Most of us have a passbook savings account, often the same one we opened when we were in school. The accounts may be nearly as old as we are—a nice thought because it gives a feeling of continuity.

Keeping records is no big deal to us and we're usually not that interested in budgets, accounting, or computerized financial planning programs. We prefer to use a more casual approach. If we have money we spend it; if not, we don't. That's not too complicated except when we're short of cash which happens fairly often. Everyone tells us we should have a budget and, even more importantly, we should balance the checkbook. We probably should but if we scrutinize our funds too much, we may be less willing to help people out financially. Most of us would feel very sad to think we didn't help someone because the budget didn't allow for it.

Clever financial planners are fond of enticing us with investments that will pay for our children's education. This is a good strategy for Ls but many of us will need help to grasp the specifics of how they work. We Ls have a serious challenge with the intricacies of insurance and investment plans. They're so overwhelming. And there's all that hype about wills and trusts. So much paperwork. So many details. Its hard to keep up with it all.

We need financial coaches to help us figure out what to do and to help us get organized. We need regular follow-up, too, so that we'll stay on top of things. It's easy for us to get sidetracked. We can't work with just any financial investor, either. We need someone who is honest and caring, and willing to invest time and effort to understand us and our issues. We need someone who'll respect our wishes and accept our slowness in making decisions. We need truthful information and patient leadership.

The E Character

Life's an adventure and I'm in the middle of everything. I thrive on excitement. I'm energized by chaos. I'm challenged by the unknown. Some people say I "live for the moment," but I think of it as going with the flow. I live life with zest, and without regret.

I'm an optimistic, sociable person. I've yet to meet someone I didn't get along with. I'm charming and witty—and not very humble. I'm interested in many things and like to be involved with lots of different people. I think Es are fun and entertaining.

I'm someone who tests limits and pushes boundaries. Why not? It's the best way to discover new possibilities. When someone tells me I can't do something, I go ahead and do it. I love to prove people wrong!

As with other Es, high drama is common in my life. I do things that might scare other people. I'm always looking for situations that stimulate my adrenaline. I excel in careers that require risk, energy, and cleverness. I'd be bored to death by predictable, routine jobs that tie me to a desk all day. I want to be challenged. I want to move around, mix with people, pull rabbits out of hats, and use my imagination. I need freedom and adventure.

Yes, I'm free-spirited and impulsive. Some people say I act childish and crazy, but I like the wildness and energy of my character. Friends tell me I burn the candle at both ends. How do I do it? It's easy. I have lots of energy and a great attitude. And I'm physically and emotionally resilient.

On a more serious note, I meet my personal problems head on. I don't waste time brooding or worrying. I just find a workable solution. I'm a down-to-earth kind of person. I'm sensible rather than theoretical. I want information that's immediately useful. People think I'm a good salesperson because I don't allow other people's reactions to affect me. I'm usually tolerant and unprejudiced, and willing to give everyone a chance.

I've been told I'm hedonistic, too focused on my own pleasure, and too extravagant in my acquisitions. I'm not denying it, but I will say that I'm also very generous and happy to share my toys. I say, do things while you can. Hey, life isn't always easy and a little fun along the way feels good.

Motivations and Goals   E

What motivates me? Challenge. Creativity. Innovation. What sparks my motiva-
tion? The needs of the moment. The possibilities of the unknown. The thrill of
adventure. Having fun. What motivates you?

In terms of goals, I'm much more interested in the process of setting them than
achieving them, though I like success as much as anybody. I guess you could say
I'm more interested in the hike than the destination. Too much structure holds me
back so I want goals that evolve as I go along. I'm comfortable with change and,
as I said before, I react to whatever's going on at the time. This keeps my goals
dynamic and interesting to me.

I'm a keep-it-simple person so I write my goals in direct, no-frills language that
anyone at any intellectual level can read. I use action words because they engage
my competitive spirit. I like the immediacy of short-range goals. My attention
wanders when I have to look too far ahead. I also set goals I'm sure I can reach.
There's no payoff in making things too hard. Success—like winning—turns me
on!

Learning   E

I'm hungry to learn, especially when I can be be creative and do things myself. I'm
a hands-on learner. I like teachers who use unusual teaching methods. I love
puzzles, games, and contests. I also love movies because they capture my imagi-
nation. Desk work drives me crazy—you know, the pencil-and-paper drills and
fill-in-the-blank questions. Dull, dull, dull. I'd rather do experiments, projects, or
demonstrations. I learn much better when I can be active and have the freedom to
figure things out for myself.

Schools have rules and that can be a problem for me. When I'm forced to sit and
be quiet, listen to longwinded lectures, or do exactly what everybody else is doing,
I get restless. I talk. I fidget. I stop paying attention. I do things that annoy others.
It's not that I try to be a behavior problem; it's just that I'm bored and want to pick
up the action. I hate sitting around doing nothing. But when teachers present
interesting, useful things in ways that relate to me, I'm filled with energy and
enthusiasm.

Communication

My specialty is communication. I love to talk. I'll talk about anything with anyone. I'm usually witty, always charming, and often the life of the party. I collect interesting stories and relish telling them with a dramatic flair. I love to use my voice and body language to create a sense of mystery, and to convince people that anything is possible. People say I'm fun to talk with.

I'm the most spirited and the most unpredictable of all the characters. My mother says I'm mysterious. People have a hard time pinning me down, or even defining me in constant ways. I'm multi-faceted. Doesn't that sound nice? I think it's one of my best traits. I also think it's what keeps me interested in myself and exciting to others.

I am a skillful mediator and negotiator. I mean that modestly. I use my sense of drama and my changeability to keep communication flowing and to feel my way toward the best resolution. The volatility and the sheer intensity of high-impact communication excites me. My focused-on-the-moment style is certainly an asset here. I'm also a talented auctioneer and salesperson. Selling is an art form and I can be very persuasive.

Whether I'm at a party or in the office, I often take an uncommitted position on the matter at hand, at least at first. I like to keep my options open. I realize this annoys people who need predictability and closure. But when decisions are made too early, it limits the opportunities for finding new ideas and solutions. Besides, I'm a great one for letting things evolve.

Life is meant to be enjoyed. I can't see why people let things get them down. I refuse to become a serious, stoic person every time I have to make a formal presentation. I approach everything with the same winning ways I use at social gatherings. So what if I'm a bit more casual and relaxed in business situations. Please don't misunderstand. I'm neither flippant nor unprepared, and I do take it all seriously. I simply like to lighten up the atmosphere and help people feel friendlier and more positive.

I'm practical and straightforward in my business dealings, and always look for expedient and feasible solutions. I won't be ensnared in schedules and picky points of detail. Practicality first and humor second—that's a formula everyone can use. A little energy and enthusiasm helps, too.

Character Studies   33

I admit it, I'm a flirt. Even so, I'm fiercely loyal to the people I care about. Whether or not I'm married, I still notice people of the opposite gender, even my own gender if the truth is told. I like to see what people wear and how they act. I notice who they're attracted to. It's so much fun!

I'm warm and friendly. I have an intimate style of camaraderie that can be confusing to people who want a deeper relationship with me. I don't mean to misrepresent myself. I respond with genuine emotion in moments that call for that kind of closeness. I don't intend to take advantage of people, nor do I mean for my "seize the opportunity" attitude to convey lack of commitment. I'm not flighty, and I'm not manipulative. When I commit to a relationship, I do so sincerely. I have many close friends. For all my closeness, though, I often keep certain thoughts and feelings to myself. I am, at heart, a private person.

I put a lot of energy into my stable relationships. While I insist on a certain amount of personal autonomy, I work hard to keep communication open. I can be exceptionally romantic. I'm a creative, innovative lover. I'm affectionate. I'm also impulsive so I may get sidetracked on the way to meet my mate at a restaurant and arrive late.

I'm the virtuoso of the grand gesture. I shower my mate, family, and friends with extravagant gifts, often delivered publicly with a flamboyant style. Once I rented a billboard to proclaim my love for my mate; another time I hired a singing messenger to deliver a dozen chocolate roses.

I open my home to everyone. I love parties and family gatherings. I like to cook exotic foods. I like to dance, play music, and indulge in all kinds of games from volleyball to charades. I especially love to play with my kids and pets. I'm a family person.

I allow for a great deal of autonomy in raising my children. I want them to be able to think and fend for themselves. I encourage them to take risks and do new things. I feel it's my duty to arm them with as many life-skills as possible. I'm very active in my children's lives and do my best to share and support their interests. I welcome advice but I set my own standards for child-raising.

Leadership and Management

People tell me I'm a good leader. They like my energy, my positive attitude, and my confidence. They also like my exceptional arbitration and diplomatic skills which allow me to accomplish seemingly impossible tasks. I'll do whatever it takes to solve a problem. I have no strong ties to the future or the past, so I adapt to new situations and methods with ease. I'm not intimidated by crises. In fact, I welcome them. Whether the issue involves labor relations, saving a business or starting a new one, I'm there to work out the kinks.

Closure and task completion are rarely priorities with me personally. I like to get the ball rolling and delegate the details to other people. I dislike being hounded by precedent, rules, or impossible deadlines. In today's market you simply have to be flexible. I'm willing to work hard and when the occasion calls for it, I can be purposeful, focused, and inexhaustible. These bursts of dedication stem more from my desire to achieve the impossible than my need to accomplish the task. Of course performance is important to me. I just prefer to take it all in stride and concentrate on what I do best.

My management strategy includes networking, acknowledging others, delegating tasks, and supporting positive action. I'm results-oriented. I'm more interested in the underlying facts of a problem and only secondarily in people's personal issues or motivations. I want to see plans and progress. I can be a bear when people drag their feet or make too many excuses. I admire and reward action and innovation.

I'm definitely not the master of written reports. I'm much better at verbal planning and decision-making. Like most Es, I need a strong O secretary or project leader to attend to reports, procedures, and schedules. I have so much going on at once that I often need a whole support staff to make sure everything is handled properly. I'm not a detail person; I'm an idea person, a troubleshooter. I'm usually the one my company sends to handle tough situations because I forsee the problems and offer practical solutions.

I manage by walking around and talking on the telephone. I need frequent contact with my employees. I notice problems early and take immediate steps to correct them. I foster ingenuity, creativity, and practicality.

If there's money in my pocket, I spend it. Exciting experiences cost money and I'm easily persuaded to plunk down the cash or credit to make them happen. Money doesn't burn a hole in my pocket and you may not find a large amount in my savings account. This isn't to say I don't save or invest. Quite the contrary. I'm just as adventurous with my financial life. If someone I respect inspires me with interesting possibilities, I'll find the capital. I'm always open to exciting opportunities.

With my quick-results, live-for-now approach to everything, I'm easily frustrated or bored with financial ventures that have no immediate action or reward. No savings bonds for me. Stocks, venture capital, start-up businesses all capture my attention and spark my ingenuity. I'm willing to take risks and regroup if things fall apart. My motto is: "Money is round and it rolls; one day I have it, the next day someone else does and the day after that, it's mine again." So why worry?

I have a varied financial portfolio. I'm prone to an eclectic mix of products ranging from precious metals to stock options. I invest in art, too. I also gamble—and not just at the poker table either. I'll bet on people if I think they have potential. What I mean is, I'll back someone who needs cash to start or expand a business, get a professional degree, or get into the financial scene in a bigger way. I do expect a return on my investment.

I'm a natural fund-raiser owing, I think, to my salesmanship and my talent for schmoozing. I think it's fun. I'm inventive and skillful. I can bluff, inspire, and cajole. In fact, I'm a great salesperson when I believe in the service or product. I can sell ideas, hope, and confidence. I sell whatever's necessary to persuade people to part with their money. I'm motivated by sales incentives and rewards. I'm optimistic and resilient so a "no" response doesn't defeat me. As I said earlier, sales is an art form and I love the challenge.

As for details, well, you know the story already. I don't do details. I don't do records. I need hands-on help from my financial advisors. I like brokers and sales agents who pay attention to me and follow through with the things I need. Good advice doesn't hurt, either.

Character Comparisons

People-watching can make the most boring event more pleasant. Whether you're listening to a dull lecture, waiting in an airport, or eating alone in a restaurant, amuse yourself with a private game of Character ID. Use the Character Comparisons in this chapter to help you identify who's who among the people around you. Soon you'll recognize someone's probable character by the things you see and hear. You'll gain useful insight into what's interesting or important to the person, and what you might do to establish rapport.

Be careful not to typecast everyone into a one-character role. To pinpoint someone as a particular character is useful only insofar as it helps you figure out how you might get to know someone better, negotiate a contract, resolve a conflict, show appreciation, and so on.

Remember that people do behave out of character at times. People may portray different characters at home and at work. They might express one character's behavior when they're feeling good, and a different one when they're upset. They may even portray one character with a particular person and another with someone else. Use the comparisons to help you get your bearings as people switch from one role to another.

The Character Comparisons will help you orient yourself to different points of view and keep you from judging everyone on the basis of yourself. This will free you to see others more clearly and give you room to respond with greater diversity, relevance, and impact.

	R	O	L	E
Mission	knowing	serving	becoming	creating
Themes	accomplishment competency	responsibility belonging	identity significance	action adventure
Roles	conceptualizer thinker visionary planner analyzer problem solver	producer organizer conservator manager supervisor stabilizer	facilitator pleaser dreamer helper harmonizer nurturer	negotiator playmate innovator adapter pioneer trouble shooter
Focus	learning	achieving	relating	doing
Needs	time to think before making decisions	purposeful activity, security, recognition	harmony with inner self, purpose in life	freedom to take immediate action
Offers	solutions	advice	feelings	options
Wants to be	well-informed respected	in control approved of	appreciated understood	liked the center of attention
Wants you to be	factual, logical, concise, precise, noninterruptive	responsible, precise, organized, on time	caring, honest, loyal, nurturing, accepting	stimulating, practical, open-minded, fun
Assets	intelligence, leadership, wit, cool-headedness	common sense, detail focus, perseverance	tolerance, patience, compassion, sincerity	comfort with change, ability to take risks
Liabilities	intolerance, sarcasm, arrogance, indifference	closed-mindedness, impatience, perfectionism	dependence on others, unassertive, smothering	capriciousness, egotism, disobedience, instability
When upset is	indecisive, critical, fault-finding, rude, aloof, uncooperative	anxious, worried, blaming, self-critical, bossy, rigid, tired, depressed	withdrawn, resentful, resistant, disheartened, overly sensitive	rude, defiant, self-indulgent, deceitful, temperamental

	R	O	L	E
Values	wisdom, integrity, justice, accuracy, curiosity, new ideas, new technology, independence	dedication, responsibility, follow-through, diplomacy, punctuality, order	authenticity, respect, truthfulness, kindness, affiliation, faithfulness, supportiveness	independence, change courage, individualism, sense of humor, new ideas, originality
Likes	learning, solitude, new experiences, time for reflection, verbal debate, being right, computers, quiet space, being fair, obscure words	plans, lists, calendars, charts, maps, policies, organization, order, punctuality, meetings, details, completion, efficiency, recognition	home and family, hugs, sharing feelings, best friends, helping others, reunions, sing-alongs, gardens, candlelight, sentimental moments	new things, outrageous friends, exotic foods, loud music, bright colors, having fun, variety, tools, moving fast, spending money, being entertained
Dislikes	group process, mundane tasks, interruptions, repetition, emotional dependence, sharing feelings, shopping	clutter, messiness, crooked pictures, noise, wasting time, rule-breakers, dirty cars, lack of courtesy, waiting	selfishness, rudeness, aggression, hostility, pressure to perform, people who take unfair advantage of others	structure, paperwork, reports, boredom, limits, discipline, organization, rank, surveillance by others, inactivity
Stressors	red tape, minutiae, incompetence, being late, illogic, deadlines, things that don't work, inaccurate information	disorder, being late, indecisiveness, missing deadlines, last-minute changes, owing money, unfinished tasks	confrontation, discord, prejudice, intolerance, adversity, being treated impersonally, being ignored, violence	rules, deadlines, details, pressure to conform, filling out forms, etiquette, being told what to do, other people's jealousy
Relaxers	experimenting with things, having time alone, working on hobbies, watching TV, listening to music reading something worthwhile	finishing things, tidying up, getting organized, planning events, making lists, finishing tasks, crafts or hobbies, reading novels or useful books	discussing things, taking a bath, listening to music, journaling, meditating, puttering, being outside, reading poetry, self-help or spiritual books	creating things, being active, having fun, going shopping, being weird, getting outside, doing crafts or hobbies, pets, reading travel guides

APPEARANCE

	R	O	L	E
Dress	conservative look neat, functional style chooses comfortable, durable clothes may use random mix of colors, styles uninterested in fashion	classical look well-coordinated style chooses appropriate clothes matching accessories, defined color schemes mix-and-match outfits	unique look soft, friendly style chooses flowing, soft lines, colors, textures personal touches and keepsake items mixes old and new styles	dramatic look innovative style chooses labels that impress others mixes bargain and designer items bold colors and styles
Body language	reserved, contained quiet manner body may be stiff planned movements little eye contact	industrious, courteous businesslike manner always doing something purposeful body motion intense eye gaze	open, inviting gentle manner uses hugs and touch quiet body motions smiles, head nodding	active, gregarious excited manner moves among people animated gestures and facial expressions
Speaking style	usually says little not much vocal variety chooses precise words uses witticism ribs others	direct, to the point moderate vocal variety chooses words for clarity discusses events likes to give advice	chatty moderate vocal variety chooses words for intent likes to share personal experiences	highly sociable lots of vocal variety selects words for impact moves among topics tells jokes and stories
General approach	steady, consistent sees the big picture holds firm if opposed analyzes and evaluates focuses on principles	predictable, firm sees the details seeks best alternatives applies rules, precedent focuses on facts	compliant, changeable sees the personal aspect yields to avoid conflict responds to values focuses on feelings	responds to the moment sees the possibilities mediates when needed finds quick solutions focuses on action
Decision making	weighs pros and cons impersonal, logical reaches decisions slowly seeks long-range view	applies rules orderly, sensible makes decisions quickly seeks closure	responds to values personal, empathetic reaches decisions slowly seeks consensus	reacts to circumstances practical, adaptive makes decisions quickly seeks solutions

ROLE Play

PATTERNS AND HABITS

	R	O	L	E
Thinking Patterns	logical thinker	sequential thinker	relational thinker	creative thinker
	analytical, conceptual	practical, factual	imaginative, personal	active, inventive
	fair, impersonal	consequential, controlled	idealistic, humane	immediate, open
Study Habits	needs facts and figures	needs practical focus	needs personal meaning	needs hands-on activity
	needs time to think	needs deadlines	needs to express ideas	needs topics to be useful
	studies best alone	studies best with a plan	studies best in groups	studies in brief spurts
	learns by challenging	learns by application	learns by discussing	learns by experience
	likes independent study, enjoys debate	likes pencil and paper exercises, visual aids	likes stories and personal examples	likes immediate application and reward
Spending Habits	prudent	cautious	altruistic	extravagant
	money means winning the game	money means security and success	money means supporting ideals	money means power and freedom to spend
	usually has well-defined financial plans	usually has savings and insurance plans	tends not to save or manage finances well	tends to win big/lose big due to risky ventures
	likes to have a broad-based portfolio with a proven record	likes safe investments, insurance policies, and income properties	likes to invest in people, art, businesses of friends or family	likes speculative deals, startup businesses, high-risk ventures
Social Habits	arrives on time	arrives early	arrives early or on time	arrives late
	stands back	keeps busy	leans forward	moves around a lot
	quietly observes others	often finds things to do	talks intently to people	often the social leader
	tends to be reserved	tends to be more serious	tends to be affectionate	tends to be impulsive
	witty communicator	focused communicator	intimate communicator	lively communicator
	usually wants to leave early	stays a proper amount of time	stays as long as feeling needed or connected	stays as long as something's happening
	looks for interesting discussions	looks for a well-planned event and good food	looks for meaningful interactions with people	looks for a good time and new adventure

	W O R K H I G H L I G H T S			
	R	**O**	**L**	**E**
Style	works well with concepts	works well with policies	works well with people	works well with chaos
	information driven	task driven	values driven	action driven
	predicts logical results	organizes people, tasks	inspires, supports people	wants direct involvement
	makes logical decisions	makes realistic decisions	makes careful decisions	makes quick decisions
	critiques others	instructs others	affirms others	stimulates
	needs to see big picture	needs to focus on details	needs to see possibilities	needs to see usefulness
	dislikes interruptions	dislikes disorder	dislikes conflict	dislikes unpleasantness
	can be rude	can be bossy	can be moody	can be volatile
	analytical, impatient	sensible, driven	idealistic, committed	optimistic, impulsive
	strives for excellence	strives for stability	strives for consensus	strives for quick results
Values	ability, justice	stability, tradition	integrity, harmony	skill, diplomacy
Strengths	vision	organization	communication skills	ability to handle chaos
	leadership	administration	team building	negotiation
Needs	quiet, autonomy	procedural structure	connection with others	freedom to create
	uninterrupted time	defined tasks, deadlines	chance to share ideas	staff to handle details
Likes	explanations, answers	sense of belonging	inspiration, nurturing	variety, excitement
	solving tough problems	getting things done	managing personnel	competing, winning
	designing and redesigning systems	managing / organizing people and projects	facilitating and supporting employees	verbal planning, short-range projects
Provides	clear analysis	advice	a listening ear	change, innovation
	effective solutions	task completion	advocacy	ability to take risks
Wants	fair treatment, respect	approval, recognition	acceptance, affirmation	attention, praise
Dreads	incompetence, confusion, emotional upheaval	loss of purpose, failure, organizational breakdown	rejection, isolation, blame and accusation	boundaries, boredom, pressing deadlines

	R	O	L	E
Style	physically and emotionally controlled	physically and emotionally composed	physically and emotionally expressive	physically and emotionally passionate
	"strong, silent" type	"friendly, efficient" type	"warm, sensitive" type	"charming, elusive" type
Attributes	ethical, independent, reasonable, stable	loyal, realistic, sensible, responsible, familial	loving, idealistic, romantic, affectionate, caring	outgoing, impulsive, optimistic, playful
Needs	respect, privacy, honesty, fairness, autonomy	fidelity, companionship, partnership, help at home	trust, intimacy, harmony, connection, romance	tolerance, participation, excitement, variety
Gives	stability	order	understanding	energy
	logical objectivity	practical common sense	emotional support	creative imagination
Shows affection	infrequently, privately, one arm/half body hug	formally, frequently, prim hug with pat on back	openly, easily, full body embrace	casually, impulsively, quick hug, slap on back
Achieves intimacy	by ideas and debating issues	by sharing everyday experiences	by sharing deepest thoughts and feelings	by doing many things together
	does not seek intimacy	expressed in actions	expresses it consistently	expresses it sporadically
	does not probe inner feelings easily	shares personal feelings when necessary	needs intimacy at all levels	does not require a deep level of intimacy
Approach to conflict	becomes cool, analytical	argues specific facts	personalizes everything	gets derailed easily
	may miss hurt feelings	looks for right and wrong	gives in quickly	sees all sides of an issue
	likes to generalize issues	sees issues simplistically	may get too emotional	hard to pin down
Dislikes	dealing with personal feelings	discussion without resolution of issues	dealing with conflict and unresolved tension	long, serious discussions, pressure to commit
	emotional outbursts	being taken for granted	being ignored	not being taken seriously
Fears	failure	disapproval	rejection	being tied down
	loss of regard, respect	loss of security	abandonment	stagnation

Character Development

People sometimes talk about feeling stuck, trapped in old patterns they'd like to change. They want to be more open, for example, or more flexible, more decisive or powerful. Some want to be better organized or more patient. Others just want to cope differently with someone or something. In other words, people want to diversify.

In the performance world, actors strive to diversify the characters they play. They seek a variety of roles that enables them to be more versatile and to avoid being typecast. We need to avoid type-casting, too. When we vary the characters we play, or even the way we play our main characters, we're better balanced, easier to get along with, more well-rounded and adapt-able.

Think about yourself for a moment. You already possess attributes that bring you personal strength and comfort, ways of thinking and behaving that speak positively about you. You may also have some traits that get in your way, that hinder your work or relationships. Wouldn't it be fun to break out of your old mold a bit and play with something new? While this phrase probably tickles the Es most, all of us are interested in personal growth and peak performance.

The goal of this chapter is self-development. The intent is for you to gain hands-on experience in doing things differently. The purpose here is to expand your options, not to re-cast you into a role that doesn't suit you.

This chapter gives you two approaches to personal development. The first focuses on your main character, adding flexibility through strategies de-signed to offset certain limitations. The second expands your ROLE by strengthening the weaker characters in your profile, using their attributes for breadth and depth. Explore both options.

Strategies for Rs

- **Pay attention to your feelings and express them more often.** Begin saying the phrase "I feel" more and "I think" less. Notice the words that convey feelings and use them.

- **Listen to other people's feelings** and accept that what they tell you is valid for them, even if you disagree.

- **Participate more fully in family and group activities.** Be an active rather than silent presence. Listen and respond more directly. Join in and do things that others like to do. Encourage them to participate in some of your activities.

- **Be more social.** Be attentive to what other people say. Do your best to share experiences, stories, and humor. You have an exceptional wit and others will appreciate it as long as you don't point it at them in a critical way.

- **Be patient and accepting of people's differences.** Everyone has special needs and skills as well as shortcomings. You will derive more benefit from people's assets than you will suffer from their liabilities. We all need each other.

- **Share your soft side.** You can admit your vulnerabilities to someone who is close to you, someone you trust. When you do this, the other person can be more open and revealing, too. This enables both of you to become emotionally closer.

- **Affirm and reward people's positive behavior**. Whether you're dealing with employees, friends, children, or your mate, most people like to have feedback, especially when it's positive. Your tendency to expect much and say little may cause you to be silent at times when a few words of praise or encouragement are needed most.

- **Be actively helpful.** Your inclination to put practical things off while you pursue your own interests may cause others to be upset with you. When action is called for, just get up and do it.

Strategies for Os

- **Be more open to new ideas and methods.** You are traditional and conservative by nature, and prefer to follow old, established beliefs and routines. Precedent is not always best, so let loose! Give yourself permission to explore and experiment more often.

- **Be more spontaneous, more adventurous.** If someone invites you to do something unexpected, say "Yes!" Take advantage of opportunities. Be flexible.

- **Accept change as a good thing.** Security is a strong motivator for you and change means a temporary loss of ability to predict and plan. Give yourself time to adjust. Once you adapt, you will feel secure again.

- **Play more.** Your tendency to put off playing until you have finished working means that you rarely get enough time to have fun. Your sense of responsibility will enable you to play more often if you insert it as a planned item in your schedule book.

- **Practice self-acceptance.** Change your wording. Use a thesaurus to find kinder, more accepting synonyms for the harsh, critical words you use to describe yourself or your behavior.

- **Share your feelings.** Your need to be self-reliant causes you to stuff your feelings rather than express them. Other people will know from your body language that something's wrong but they won't know what it is. It's easier on everyone when you say what's on your mind.

- **Smile more often, give more hugs.** You tend to be too serious and too formal. People will notice your warmth and friendliness when you relax, smile, and act in more affectionate ways.

- **Delegate.** Accept that most people want to do a good job. Trust that they'll get things done in their own way and within a time schedule that you agree upon together. People perform better this way. Be more lenient.

Strategies for Ls

- **Be more assertive.** Learn to say "no" and say it whenever you need to protect your boundaries. Your desire to avoid conflict causes you to be so lenient with people that they really don't know when they've exceeded your limits or patience.

- **Be more objective.** Your habit of taking things too personally clouds your ability to hear and respond to others fairly. To clear up potential misunderstanding, paraphrase what you heard and check its meaning with the person who said it.

- **Spend time doing your own thing.** You need to have time for personal growth and development. Too much togetherness or caring for others can cause emotional exhaustion and depletion. Your inner well-being requires some high-quality alone time.

- **Be accepting of disagreement.** When people are able to air and resolve their differing ideas and viewpoints, everyone wins. When there isn't a ready agreement or solution, let people deal with it in their own way. Remember you are not solely responsible for everyone's feelings. Besides, people grow most when they have to work out the difficulties themselves.

- **Be more practical.** When it comes to being practical, take a page from the O's book. Make a list of things that must be done and get busy doing them. Even if you finish only one task, you'll feel so much better afterward!

- **Face today's problems today.** Don't wait for inspiration. When you need help or a decision from someone in order for you to get started, ask for it right away. The longer you wait, the harder it is to ask for help. People are usually willing to help, especially when you show appreciation.

- **Refrain from offering unsolicited help.** People need to feel they can manage their own problems. Trust that when they need your help, they'll ask for it. When you offer help too soon or too often, it robs others of their autonomy.

Strategies for Es

- **Follow through on tasks.** You're best known for your jack-rabbit starts and your short attention span on long-range projects. Set up some checkpoints you can commit to. Hire someone to help if needed. View the follow-through aspects as a playful challenge.

- **Stay in one place longer.** Take frequent breaks if needed. Vary your routine to prevent boredom or frustration. Talk to people at regular intervals to ward off isolation.

- **Be more accountable**. People need to know how to reach you and what to expect. Call in at scheduled times when people can't reach you by phone. Be on time or call if you'll be late. Set reasonable plans with realistic deadlines.

- **Develop more discipline.** Make a list of necessary tasks and check them off as you do them. Better yet, tie your completion to tangible rewards you can give yourself when you've finished each task.

- **Practice yoga, meditation, and deep breathing.** Quieting activities will help you get a grip and relax the daily tensions that make you edgy. Use music, creative hobbies, journaling, hot baths, and massages to help you unwind.

- **Be more reflective.** Take walks or long drives in the car. Engage in hobbies that offer reflective time such as gardening, fishing, hiking, or jigsaw puzzles. They will help you step back and take a broader, deeper look at yourself. Your tendency to be busy may otherwise cause you to miss the forest for the trees.

- **Develop more focus—do one task at a time.** You are very skilled at juggling many tasks or people at once, a process that brings you challenge and excitement. The downside is you may become too scattered to meet anyone's needs effectively. Limit how much you take on and use a calendar to keep track of your commitments if needed.

ROLE Expansion

Until now, we've concentrated on developing your main character. But suppose you'd like to be more daring, to step even further out of character by adopting a different frame of reference. Actors do this all the time when they take on a new role. Why not have some fun with this approach?

Let's begin with the understanding that you, like the rest of us, are multi-dimensional. That is, you have four distinct characters in your profile. The look and feel of your strongest character is directly affected by which character is second, third, and fourth. This is what separates one R, for instance, from other Rs. Though some characters are obviously better developed than others, you still have all of their potential strengths—and limitations—at your disposal.

Each character has its own special gifts. Here are a few highlights.

R supplies the framework.

> It adds clarity, objectivity, reasoning ability, and conceptual vision. It helps you set logical goals, use sound judgment, and make fair decisions. R gives you clear thinking.

O supplies the focus.

> It adds orderliness, realism, structure, and responsibility. It brings you patience for details, a common-sense approach, and the ability to get things done. O gives you efficiency.

L supplies the feeling.

> It adds kindness, sensitivity, idealism, and connectedness. It helps you revere people and relationships, affirm others, and be true to life's meaning. L gives you passion.

E supplies the fun.

> It adds energy, spunk, innovation, and change. It enables you to see things creatively, focus on the moment, take risks, and be more carefree. E gives you resilience.

Why not use these gifts to help you do things in ways that are unusual for you? When you strengthen latent abilities you have but don't use, you can be far more flexible than ever before, and more resourceful than you can imagine.

Turn to page 9 and review your character profile. Write the letters in here, the strongest character on the left; the weakest on the right: ___ ___ ___ ___. Choose a character you want to develop. Read on.

Rational

- **Start with the big picture first.**
  Draw up a conceptual plan; put it on paper so you can see it.

- **Do your homework.**
  Gather information, check facts, prepare confirming data.

- **Analyze your information.**
  Do a pro-and-con analysis of all factors before making decisions.

- **Have a contingency plan.**
  Prepare for the unexpected with alternative options.

- **Focus on priorities.**
  Do the highest priority tasks first.

Organized

- **Make a "to do" list.**
  Write each thing you want to do and check it off when it's done.

- **Do one thing at a time.**
  Start and finish one task before beginning another.

- **Get started right away.**
  Get everything you need yourself—don't depend on others.

- **Keep busy.**
  There is always something useful you can do, even hobbies.

- **Center yourself.**
  Re-focus with stabilizing rituals such as deep breathing, hot baths, exercise, journaling, organizing or cleaning something.

Loving

- **Spend more time with other people.**
  Be aware of your emotions, share feelings, develop empathy.
- **Be more understanding and accepting.**
  Allow time and patience for your interactions with others.
- **Do things for others.**
  Help on projects, do volunteer work, focus on others.
- **Be more open.**
  Smile more, make eye contact, give hugs, listen more.
- **Notice and affirm others.**
  Give support and praise, give cards or notes at special times.

Energized

- **Play more.**
  Be more social, go on trips, develop new interests, play games.
- **Break up your old routine.**
  Explore new ideas, activities, people, and places.
- **Be more spontaneous.**
  Hide your calendar on weekends, say "Yes!" to invitations.
- **Be creative.**
  Take music lessons, learn a language, find a new hobby.
- **Daydream.**
  Just let your mind expand.

What you do with this list probably depends on which character is operating most strongly. Es will dabble in everything that interests them. Ls will want to flow with whatever feels right. Rs may spend more time contemplating than doing. Os will focus on one character at a time so they don't become too scattered. What about you?

Don't worry about losing yourself—your special characteristics and abilities—while you experiment with another characters' attitudes and behavior. Simply use them to explore new options and to enhance, not replace, who you are. This is an easy way to have some fun and learn a lot.

Acting Out of Character

When actors step into a new role, they often work from the outside in, using images and stage directions to transport themselves into a new frame of reference. Most actors practice behaving in ways quite different from their own in order to become comfortable and spontaneous with their characters' responses. Actors know that when they behave differently, they think differently; when they think differently, they act differently.

This same process will work for you. Whether you choose to "flex" your main character or develop your weaker ones, the method is simple. Read the strategies that apply to you. Highlight the ones with the greatest appeal. Write them on an index card for quick reference. Practice them daily.

If you're using the ROLE expansion approach and stepping into another character, look for living role models to watch, listen to, and emulate. Read the relevant Character Study so you can immerse yourself in the language and mindset. Review the Character Comparisons for tidbits of useful information. Then go someplace your developing character might find interesting and let yourself "walk in your character's shoes." For even better results, choose a place where no one knows you. There's no opposition to differences in your behavior, and it gives you a safe place to practice. This is a technique called *role rehearsal* and it's a great way to bring your character portrayal to life!

What would the characters say about all of this? Let's find out. See if you can figure out who's talking.

Why would I want to do this? What will I gain by doing things that make me uncomfortable? I don't like parlor games and that's what this appears to be.

I don't see this as a parlor game. I can identify lots of practical reasons for doing things differently, but acting out of character isn't comfortable for me either. I like my old ways. Still, I could read the first section and apply some of those ideas.

I believe the really valuable lessons of this chapter will be obvious once we begin to experience how it feels to think and act differently. I know I'll have a much better understanding of other people when I'm able to see things from their point of view.

This sounds like fun to me, especially the role rehearsal part! I'd much rather do something with these ideas than sit around and talk them to death. I'm going to get some new clothes to fit my new image, and maybe some new props, too. Let's see, do I have my charge card with me?

You're always looking for an excuse to play! This is a serious exercise.

I know, but can't we have fun anyway? Why do you have to be so stuffy about it? I don't mean to be offensive but I think every one of you will get more out of this by just jumping in and doing it.

I don't jump into anything without forethought. That's what gets people into trouble.

I can see Erin's point, though. The more we do, the more we learn. All I need is a list and I'll be set. I like the index card idea. That's just like the cue cards actors use to remember their lines. What a great way to keep track of things. It will help me stay focused.

I know what I'm going to do. There's a get-together at my friend Lynne's house and I won't know anyone there. It'll be a wonderful place to watch and listen. Maybe I'll practice a little. Lynne won't mind. She's a lot like you, Erin. She's always doing something different.

I just got a memory flash! My grandmother used to say, "If you always do what you've always done, you'll always get what you always got." It's a corny saying but it does apply, don't you think?

There's a clear message here: Try doing something new. Whatever your favorite learning style has been, this chapter gives you a great opportunity to do things differently. So get into the act in any way you can and enjoy the show!

Reaching Out

Wouldn't you agree that you understand someone best when you speak the same language? While this is certainly true when you talk with people of different nationalities, it is equally relevant when you interact with someone who thinks, feels, and acts in ways that are unlike your own.

Suppose you want to talk with someone whose character is very different—even opposite—from yours. What you say and, even more importantly, how you say it makes a crucial difference in how well you transmit your message. When you understand and use someone else's frame of reference, that person can grasp your message more clearly. People are more receptive, more open to what you say, when your behavior allows them to feel comfortable.

The goal of communication is to be understood. This involves more than simple word choice and language pattern. It includes verbal mannerisms, facial expression, and body language.

Most of us communicate in ways that fit us. We choose actions and presentation styles that make sense to us, ones we most readily understand. Watch and listen carefully as people speak and you'll get useful clues about each person's preferred approach.

Nowhere are the nuances of communication more important than when we're trying to impress, convince, persuade, seduce, cajole, or otherwise influence someone else. Isn't this what effective sales is all about? Whether we're exchanging ideas, bargaining for the best price, mediating conflicts, presenting information, pitching products, selling ourselves, or working toward consensus, we are trying to encourage others to accept our point of view. Our styles may vary but our goal is the same.

The act of selling is all around us. Listen to a teenager explain why he was late, or "forgot" to do something. Watch a child persuade a parent to buy a coveted toy. Listen to a driver plead innocent to a traffic ticket. Notice people's dating behavior in a nightclub. Selling is not limited to auto dealerships and TV commercials. We all sell something and we do it all day long.

Do you think the ability to influence others comes more easily to certain characters? Admittedly, some are naturally more gregarious than others; some are naturally more forceful. Some have an easy way with people that instills comfort and trust. And some are more convincing by their knowledge than their actions. Every character brings something important to the interchange.

Whether we're selling products or ideas, services or ourselves, we must look beyond our own needs to properly respond to someone else's. While Ls do this most naturally, we can all learn to put ourselves in other people's shoes. Only then can we adjust our style, content, and wrapup to be in sync with other people's values and views. This allows the interchange to be more cooperative than competitive. And whether or not a successful sale occurs, the connection between people remains open for future transactions.

All this is great information but I'm not about to get into someone else's psyche in order to explain a proposal. It's not my style.

Aren't you being melodramatic? We just need to figure out someone's character and follow the appropriate protocol. The Character Comparisons will help with the ID and this chapter has all kinds of guidelines to use.

Both of you are so impersonal. What about the people themselves? I can't watch someone being treated impersonally. You have to take time to listen and talk, to build rapport.

Talk. That's great for starters but you have to close a deal. That requires finesse, a little inspiration, maybe a gift or two, and definitely some flashy persuasion. The bottom line is what counts most.

While all of you are talking, I'm going to read the rest of this chapter and then find different characters to practice with.

Convincing Rs

- Decide what you want to say in advance and get to the point quickly. Don't ramble or try to sort things out as you go along.

- Present the big picture first, then provide the important details.

- Know your facts and be willing to assemble additional data as needed to satisfy an R's wish for accurate, in-depth information.

- Be objective and factual in your approach. List the pros and cons of each alternative.

- Hold firm when you are challenged. Show self-assurance and confidence by facial expression, tone of voice, and body posture.

- Admit when you don't know something; don't try to bluff your way through it.

- Give Rs plenty of time to study the information you've provided before you expect a response.

- Encourage conversation by being logical and steady, and by asking open-ended questions. Listen respectfully and quietly.

- Be calm and direct. Being overly familiar, too excitable, or excessively dramatic makes Rs feel uncomfortable.

- Avoid making hasty revisions or snap decisions. Rs dislike disorder and rapid change.

- Don't assume that feelings and emotions are unimportant. Position them as facts to be accounted for in making decisions.

- Show appreciation for the R's vision, capabilities, and ideas. Acknowledge the R's fairness and integrity.

- Use reason and humor when challenging an R's unrealistic demands or expectations.

- Respect the R's need for privacy. This includes time, ideas, and possessions.

- Avoid letting rules, traditions, or personal biases get in the way of achieving maximum results.

Persuading Os

- Be punctual. Organize your ideas and present them directly and forcefully. Have contingency plans available.

- State your bottom line issues in clear terms. Pay attention to details.

- Document why your ideas make sense. Describe the successful applications and the benefits. Reduce the obstacles to using it.

- Be ready to take on responsibility. Stay with the given task until it is completed.

- Define the costs and benefits of your proposals. State the principles involved. Emphasize the O's good sense.

- Be orderly. Define and use procedural steps. Be attentive to standard operating procedures. Respect deadlines.

- Accept that Os need to give opinions and advice.

- Assess how much work Os already have before giving them new projects. Allow enough time to complete current tasks.

- Praise diligence, hard work, loyalty, and perseverance. Be patient with the O's affinity for detail.

- Os need to belong. Include them in the discussion, decision-making, planning, and implementation of a project.

- Help Os keep themselves from getting bogged down with too much detail. Show them the bigger picture.

- Alert Os to impending changes. Give them time to adjust before going too deeply into discussion about it.

- Help Os acquire necessary skills or modify their assignments according to their skill level.

- Permit Os to have some control over tasks and projects.

- Discuss achievements and results. To Os, this is not bragging—it is important confirmation of ability.

Influencing Ls

- Be open and friendly in your approach. Smile. Make eye contact. Keep an open body posture. How you look, sound, and behave is more important than what you say.

- Be more personal than factual. Discuss experiences, feelings, and beliefs. Ls cannot be persuaded with facts alone.

- Allow ample time for discussion of issues and feelings. Be open to the L's ideas and point of view.

- Show empathy by presenting areas of agreement first.

- Explain how your proposal is helpful and why it's the "right" thing to do. State the future benefits.

- Show why your idea is valuable to people. Name others who also support your proposal.

- Listen fully before starting to argue.

- Suggest and recommend rather than tell or demand. Be gentle when you are correcting or rejecting an idea or proposal.

- Help Ls set priorities by using their own subjective criteria, and by setting realistic due dates on specific tasks.

- Give personal expressions of appreciation with words, cards, special mementos.

- Avoid treating Ls impersonally or rudely. Show kindness and consideration. Help them express feelings and sort out conflicts.

- Be careful not to appear too arrogant. You can be passionate about your idea or proposal, but do it with humility and restraint. Be open to discussion.

- Inspire the L's imagination. Cultivate anticipation.

- Recognize unique contributions. Show appreciation for the L's feelings and ideas.

- Avoid conflict wherever possible. Look for caring ways to raise and discuss points of disagreement.

Impressing Es

- Get to the point right away and don't ramble. Avoid getting stuck in unimportant details.

- Present your ideas clearly and be ready to take immediate action.

- Make your decisions quickly. Don't waste time.

- Be lenient in your approach. Avoid being too rule-bound or restrictive. Allow freedom of ideas and expression.

- Be willing to take over parts of a project that require detail, concentration, and time.

- Be enthusiastic. Show optimism and energy in your language, facial expression, and body motions.

- Express your feelings quickly. Don't go on and on about things.

- Be friendly and sociable. Smile. Make eye contact. Be animated.

- Explore new ideas with an open mind. If you are too critical or too closed, Es won't bring innovative suggestions to you.

- When appropriate, help Es think procedurally about their projects; help them anticipate consequences and plan ahead.

- Wherever possible make the experience fun. Use stories, jokes, or intriguing hands-on activities.

- Praise the E's ingenuity and creativity.

- Enjoy the E's nontraditional ideas and focus.

- Accept the E's need for freedom and lack of constraint in setting personal work habits.

- Rely on the E's energy, endurance, and incredible sense of timing.

- Bring things for Es to see and do.

- Identify the E's motivators and set up a reward system that is connected with job duties or performance goals

Wrap Up

Now that you're practically through the *ROLE Play* book, you know there's a lot of information to absorb and apply. The big question now is: What will I do with it? The answer is: That depends.

If you simply want to have fun with the concepts and experiment a little:

- Give the First Impression Quiz and Character Cards to your family, friends, and co-workers. People love to figure out who they are, who you are, and how all of you can get to know each other better—and get along better, too.

- Have a *ROLE Play* party. Give everyone a chance to figure out who they are with the First Impression Quiz and the Character Cards. Make up your own scenarios ahead of time and get people into the action, using colored hats or costume items to represent their characters. Then have people switch roles and act out the scenario again as a different character.

If you want to determine the probable orientation and preferences of your clients in order to communicate more effectively:

- Use the First Impression Quiz and Character Cards . Ask people to do the quiz and look at the cards. Suggest they give the cards and a copy of the quiz to their family and friends.

- Observe their appearance and behavior. Listen to their voice and language patterns. Make a few notes for yourself.

- Go to the Character Studies and review the descriptions.

- Use the Character Comparisons to confirm your impressions and identify key words or concepts to write on an index card for quick reference. This will be your Cue Card.

- Refer to the Reaching Out guidelines to help you choose the approach best suited to your clients' preferences.

- Prepare Cue Cards with key words, phrases, and actions to help you communicate most effectively.

- Experiment and revise your Cue Cards as needed to fine tune your approach. Store the cards in your clients' files.

If you want to learn more about a person you might hire, appoint to a committee or board, or serve as a member of your special team:

- Use the Second Look Quiz to give you a quick, useful, and accurate appraisal of the person's personality profile, from the strongest type to the weakest. Then you can determine whether the person will fit well within the setting, bring the desired mix of personal attributes, or have the potential to succeed with the challenges of the position.

If you're engaged in the dating, mating, parenting arena and want to understand and interact more comfortably with your partner:

- Begin with the First Impression Quiz and Character Cards. Share your observations about yourselves and each other.

- Go through the *ROLE Play* book together, a little at a time, and discuss your viewpoints, feelings, and impressions.

- Use the Character Comparisons and Reaching Out chapters for guidance. Make Cue Cards for reference.

- Explore. Experiment. Revise. And practice, practice, practice!

If you're involved in employee relations, staff development, team building, or sales training, order the *ROLE Play* Leader's Guide. You'll receive all the information and materials you need to conduct effective seminars and workshops on your own. Or contact the publisher directly to hire a skilled trainer to do the teaching for you. Either way, the *ROLE Play* concepts and materials can help you help others be more understanding, accepting, responsive, and effective in their interactions with one another.

Order extra copies of the First Impression Quiz, Character Cards, and ROLE Play book directly from the publisher. The address and telephone number are in the front of the book, behind the title page.

Backstage

C'mon backstage now and hang out with us for a while. We've been chatting about our impressions and experiences with ROLE Play.

Say hi to our guest, everyone.

Hi.

As I was saying, you've all been great and I'm going to miss you. This has been a valuable experience for me and I've appreciated everyone's sincerity and honesty. It's been wonderful getting to know each of you.

Larry, you're sweet to say that. I agree with you. I feel like I have a whole new set of friends right here.

You're both so mushy, always looking for the personal touch. I think the program's been a blast. And, wow, what great insight!

You're right, Erin. I'll study the book again and type up my margin notes.

What are margin notes?

They're the notes I made in the margins of the book. You know, insights, comments, ideas, things like that. I learn best when I write things down.

You're so organized, Olga. I admire you but I can honestly say I'd never take the time to type up anything. That's why I have a secretary. Ha-ha.

Elliott, you're impossible! You're not nearly as goofy as you try to make us think you are. But if you don't study it, how will you learn it?

I did learn it, didn't you? What were all those exercises we did together?

They were class exercises to practice with. You know, role rehearsal. The practice-makes-perfect part of our learning experience.

You have an answer for everything, Olga. Those exercises gave me insight but I felt put on the spot with some of them. I saw all of you watching me every time someone mentioned the R traits of detachment and sarcasm. I don't take things too personally, but I did feel judged by each of you.

Oh, Roger, I'm so sorry. I didn't mean to hurt your feelings. I think you've just taken a big step forward by stating how you feel. Would you have done that before we started this program?

Probably not. But learning in this way has been more difficult for me, I think, than for any of you.

You aren't the only one people stare at. I've been watched by everyone my whole life because they think I'm crazy. Don't laugh, it's true. Remember the movie, Walk on the Wild Side? The title fits me, don't you think?

You are crazy, Erin, but in the nicest way. You've done so much to make this experience fun for all of us. The props, the music, the pillows for our pillow fight. I'll never forget that! And the way you talked us into making pizzas at midnight because you were hungry.

About the staring—I'm sorry if I offended anyone, especially you, Roger.

It's OK, Larry. People have always found me to be sort of odd.

You aren't odd, but you are kind of intimidating. I mean, you always know everything. You knew how to fix the computer and the video camera. You disarmed the alarm system when we came into the studio after hours. And you were so cool when the guard asked you all those questions.

Careful, Larry, you'll embarrass him.

Getting Personal

You're quiet, Olga, what's wrong?

Just thinking. People always tell me how uptight and prudish I am. I hear I'm too serious, a workaholic, and not much fun unless I'm on vacation. I didn't understand what they meant, but now I do. I have been staring at every one of you, but it's because you're becoming my role models. I love the way Erin tosses her head when she disagrees with something and then laughs. It lightens the mood. I respect the way Roberta sits back and listens until she has something valuable to say. And Lettie's so affirming, so accepting of all of us, even me.

Wait a minute, Olga. What's this "even me" stuff? I want you to know how much I appreciate the way you approach things. You're so practical and resourceful. You've kept us all on track. I've needed your common sense to keep me grounded. You know how flighty I can be.

Thanks, Erin. But I know I'm way too serious for my own good. I need to learn to lighten up. Maybe there's a book I can read to help me.

That's the problem, Olga. What you're asking for doesn't come in a book. It comes from going along with our practical jokes, or not worrying about what someone will say because we're baking pizzas at midnight. I think it really comes from living in the moment.

It's easy for you to say that, Elliott, because you do all of that very easily. But spontaneity isn't everyone's strong suit. I think Olga has been very brave to tell us how she feels and I, for one, applaud her.

Thanks for that friendly pat on the back, Roberta. That's a different style for you and I like it.

Hey, Roberta, is it time for a group hug? Just joking.

All joking aside, I think differently about that after being in ROLE Play. I see how important it is to be supportive.

Look how much we've learned to accept one another. I don't always understand your humor, Elliott, but I find myself laughing anyway. And Roger's witticisms are usually over my head but I like that he tries to be funny.

Haven't you figured out Roger's humor yet, Larry? It's usually snide. I made a list one day of all his comments about the group exercises. There were some rare thoughts there!

That's not fair, Owen. I was feeling awkward and baiting is what I do to cover up my feelings. It wasn't meant to be personal. I think I've improved a lot.

You have, but I think there's a different issue.

Shifting Focus

We're all entitled to be who we are. We need to accept each other's differences and look underneath to figure out what's really going on.

In other words, let's focus on the good inside each of us.

Bravo, Larry!

Well, it is the message of ROLE Play, isn't it?

Yes, but there's also a message about possibilities for each of us. For being able to reach inside to bring up our less dominant traits and identify what we need to be more balanced ...

And to use other characters as role models.

Yes, Erin, that too. I've been thinking about the roles I've had to play as a child, a parent, a friend. I've even thought how different I am with certain people. Can I really be two different people?

You must have missed the part about our being a rainbow—a complete spectrum of all characters. I even have a little bit of Olga in me.

I've never seen your office look organized, Lettie. There can't be too much O there!

Looking Deeper

Oh, I have my moments, Owen. I'll write up my margin notes, just like Olga. But going deeper, don't you think the life scripts we play come from our personality types?

How so?

Each of us is born with a personality profile, right? Then our life circumstances require us to use it in different ways. Look, my parents died when I was in grade school. I was sent from one relative's home to another, six months at a time, so no one would feel burdened with an extra child. I bet how I handled all that had more to do with my character than anything. Larry, if you had the same life situation, how would you have handled it?

I'd like to think I'd have seized the chance to know my relatives better, to get closer to them. To be honest, I probably would have felt unloved and abandoned with each move. I'd still be an emotional mess!

What a tough experience for you, Lettie. I think I'd have felt I had to be the best little girl in the world. I'd have followed everyone's rules to the letter. That way

I'd fit in and feel as though I belonged. I'd help with the chores so they'd keep me around. Just the thought of it makes me feel uptight!

I know what you mean. I wouldn't have been so practical. I probably would have buried myself in books and schoolwork. I'd have been so emotionally removed, so protective of my feelings that I might have stayed that way all my life.

I'd have gone to my books, like Roberta. But I'd probably have been the school activist, up to my neck in after-school clubs, the school newspaper, maybe even student office, just to have a sense of belonging somewhere.

Well, I know what I'd have done—made a lot of friends at each place and never been home. I'd have been a wild woman, no one to report to, no one to kiss up to.

Sounds brave, Erin, but I bet you'd have felt as awful as the rest of us.

Yeah, but I figure it's up to me to make my own life.

Would you have run away?

Maybe, but probably not until high school. What scares me about that situation is how easy it would have been for me to fall in with the wrong crowd. I can imagine me using every substance from pot to booze.

Would you have done that to act out or to reduce the emotional pain?

Both. I think that's why lots of kids get started with drugs. I shudder to think that could have been me. What did you do, Lettie?

I cried a lot. I kept pictures of my parents with me all the time. I had no brothers or sisters so I really felt alone. Some relatives were more caring than others. My aunt gave me a kitten and I kept Fluffy for twelve years. I'd have been lost without her. I know I have some scars, still. That's why I volunteer with homeless kids.

What a story! How did we get into this, anyway?

We were talking about our character profiles and our life scripts.

And you, reader? How would you have dealt with Lettie's situation?

Lightening Up

Say, what about that movie we saw last night?

I loved the final chase through hyperspace. Nothing like spaceships colliding to get the sparks flying.

Sorry, Elliott, I couldn't get into it. It didn't make sense that a terrorist could hack into a computer program without someone noticing. Maybe if the hero hadn't wasted so much time on the woman, he'd have noticed.

How can you say that, Roger? The romance was the best part of the movie. It broke my heart when she was carried off by cannibals.

Lettie, you're too much. I'm hungry. Anyone want to get some dinner?

Sure. Where do you want to eat?

Let's go to the Italian bistro on the corner. Agreed?

Having Fun

I have to tell you I used to get so uptight whenever we went out to eat together. You know how orderly I am and we're so unruly. Someone's always late ...

Sorry to interrupt, Olga, but remember the time Elliott was an hour late? He had a great story. Something about his motorcycle breaking down and being rescued by this blonde babe, but first they had to go to her house so she could get her keys.

I remember. That's part of it. We're all so different. Roberta wants a salad, Roger wants a burger. Larry is a vegetarian. Lettie loves ethnic foods. Erin wants spicy foods. I complain about the menu, Owen groans about the price. And Elliott goes ballistic when we nit-pick over how big a tip to leave. Aren't we fun?

Funny but true, Olga. Remember our first meal together?

How could I forget? Roger and I were the first to arrive—early of course. I complained about everyone being late and Roger calmly said, "Just because we're early doesn't mean everyone else is late." He's always so rational.

Yeah, and then there was the time he got brave and ordered veal instead of his usual burger.

Lettie lost it, carrying on about eating baby animals. Then they got into this big debate over animal rights and the inhumanity of man. Of course, Roger refused to feel guilty about being at the top of the food chain. It was a great meal!

My favorite was the time Erin tipped the waiter to bring a birthday cake to Owen so we could sing "Happy Birthday" and blow paper horns.

I was so embarrassed. It wasn't even my birthday and I hate to be stared at.

But you handled it superbly. You laughed. You made a speech. And you insisted that since it was your birthday, we should pay for your meal which we did, if you remember.

I did have fun. We all did. We're quite an entertaining group of people. Sometimes I wish I could sit on the outside and watch us in action.

And miss out on the fun? I'd much rather be in the middle of things.

Thinking Ahead

I think we should have a monthly get-together so we can keep in touch, and reinforce our growing flexibility and tolerance for people's differences.

Great idea. I'm going to prepare for our next one by getting a word-a-day calendar so I can keep up with Roberta's awesome vocabulary.

I'm going to use what I've learned here at work. I have some employee problems to deal with and I'm sure my ROLE Play training will help me.

I need to prepare a speech for my next Toastmaster's meeting. I think I'll talk about us, and try to impersonate Elliott. Hey, El, can I borrow some clothes and a few props?

Sure. Can I watch? In fact, why don't we all go and cheer you on.

How do you feel about that, Owen?

I might be more nervous with all of you there, but we've been through so much already. I think I'll be OK with it.

Isn't this meeting at 6:30 in the morning?

It's worth getting up for, Roberta. We can get some breakfast afterward.

Where's our waiter? We need our bill.

There's a Midnight Madness sale going on at the mall. Do any of you charming people want to come with me?

I'll go.

Me, too. Sounds like fun.

Owen's got the calculator. Let's figure out the tip.

Who's driving? It's silly for us to take separate cars. Besides, think of the gas we'll save by going together.

That's a new angle for you, Larry. I thought you cared more about the environment than money.

I'm learning to broaden my focus.

Great answer! Let's go.

We wish you could come too, reader. But look for us. We'll be around.

About the Author

Julie Waltz Kembel, M.S. Ed., CHES

Julie is the education director of the Health & Healing Center at Canyon Ranch health and fitness resort in Tucson, Arizona. A certified health education specialist, counselor, and clinical hypnotherapist, Julie designs programs and teaching materials and provides personal instruction in many areas of habit and lifestyle change. In addition, Julie is an adjunct clinical instructor in the University of Arizona departments of Psychology and Family and Community Medicine.

Julie holds bachelor's and master's degrees in special education from Wayne State University in Detroit, Michigan. Her 28 years of professional experience includes 13 years with the Department of Psychiatry and Behavioral Sciences, University of Washington, Seattle; three years in hospital administration; nine years at Canyon Ranch; and five years in public school classrooms.

Julie has conducted many training seminars for dietitians, physicians, nurses, dentists, and social workers, served as a consultant to business and health care organizations, appeared regularly on local and regional television and radio programs, and maintained a private counseling practice. She presently serves on the National Advisory Board of *Vitality* magazine.

Julie is the author of *Winning the Weight and Wellness Game, No Ifs, Ands, or Butts: A Smoker's Guide to Kicking the Habit*, and *Food Habit Management*, all in student and instructor editions. Additionally, Julie's written numerous manuals and workbooks, journal articles, and a variety of stories and poems on many different topics.

Other Wellness Books by Julie Waltz Kembel

Winning the Weight and Wellness Game

The award winning, comprehensive and practical guide with an innovative twist. Focuses on habits and change, food management, exercise, relaxation, overall health and wellness. May be used individually or as part of a program. The emphasis is on individualized, flexible plans. Unique Game Plan encourages planning and tracking. Easy-to-read style with amusing anecdotes and stories. 336 pages, 7" by 9" paperback.

#WIN-STD $17.95
#WIN-PLAN Extra Game Plan $1.25

Winning the Weight and Wellness Game: Instructor Guide

The instructor's manual takes the work out of setting up your own weight and wellness program. Contains information on assessment, program planning and design, special program adaptations, guidelines for individual and group instruction, chapter outlines, and a wealth of dynamic lesson enhancements. 296 pages, 8.5" by 11", comb bound for ease of use.

#WIN-INST $39.95

No Ifs, Ands, or Butts: A Smoker's Guide To Kicking The Habit

This unique book provides a comprehensive look at the physiological, psychological, emotional, and behavioral aspects of smoking cessation. Includes relapse prevention and recovery, weight control, and exercise. Contains a novella with six characters to enhance the readability. May be used individually or as part of a stop smoking program. 368 pages, 7" by 9" paperback.

#SM-STD $15.95

No Ifs, Ands, or Butts: Instructor Guide

The companion instructor's manual offers practical guidelines for program design, implementation, and marketing. Presents innovative adaptations for individual and group instruction. Includes worksheets, masters for transparencies or handouts, and detailed chapter outlines. 272 pages, 8.5" by 11" comb bound for ease of use.

#SM-INST $39.95